Remember More

Your Complete Guide to

Remembering Names, Increase Memory Retention, and Focusing Better

James Stephenson

© **Copyright 2019 - All rights reserved.**

The content contained within this book may not be reproduced, duplicated or transmitted without direct written permission from the author or the publisher.

Under no circumstances will any blame or legal responsibility be held against the publisher, or author, for any damages, reparation, or monetary loss due to the information contained within this book, either directly or indirectly.

Legal Notice:

This book is copyright protected. It is only for personal use. You cannot amend, distribute, sell, use, quote or paraphrase any part, or the content within this book, without the consent of the author or publisher.

Disclaimer Notice:

Please note the information contained within this document is for educational and entertainment purposes only. All effort has been executed to present accurate, up to date, reliable, complete information. No warranties of any kind are declared or implied. Readers acknowledge that the author is not engaging in the rendering of legal, financial, medical or professional advice. The content within this book has been derived from various sources. Please consult a licensed professional before attempting any techniques outlined in this book.

By reading this document, the reader agrees that under no circumstances is the author responsible for any losses, direct or indirect, that are incurred as a result of the use of information contained within this document, including, but not limited to, errors, omissions, or inaccuracies.

Table of Contents

Introduction

Chapter 1 - Welcome to Your Mind!

...The Inner Workings of Your Mind

The Pattern of Predictions

What Is Memory?

Based on Types

Based on Stages

Memory Process

Encoding

Storage

Retrieval

Can We Really Enhance Our Memory?

Chapter 2: Memory Basics that Everyone Needs to Know to Before Brain Training

Test #1

Test #2

Test #3

Points Tally

Expert

Average

Untrained

How Do You Train Your Memory?

The Basic Terms of Memory Processes

Stimuli

- Neurological
- Synapses
- Perception
- Recall
- Engram
- Active Processing
- Cognition

What Elements Affect Your Memory?
- Retention Ability
- Good Health
- Age
- Will to Remember
- Meaningful Material
- Proper Sleep

Why Do We Forget Things in the First Place?
- Failure in Retention
- Interference
- Storage Problems
- Intentional Forgetfulness

The Power of the Human Memory

Chapter 3 – Understanding Your Mind: What Does Your Brain Really Love?

The Different Types of Brain Waves
- Infra-low: <.5Hz

    Delta Waves: .5 to 3 Hz

    Theta Waves: 3 to 8 Hz

    Alpha Waves: 8 to 12 Hz

    Beta Waves: 12 to 38 Hz

    Gamma Waves: 38 to 42 Hz

Memory Preferences

Neuroplasticity and How It Affects the Mind

Chapter 4 - The Mindset of a Memory Genius: What They Do and How They Do It

The Mindset of Successful Memory Athletes

    Train, Train, Train

    Improve Your Goals

    Surround Yourself with People Who Motivate You

    Watch Your Diet

Change Is Not Instant

The Law of Averages

Chapter 5 – Forgetting and Improving Memory

Why Your Hippocampus Creates Memories and Erases Them

Misidentification of Facts

The Decay Process

Distractions

Chapter 6 – Information Overload

Overload and Its Toll on Memory

Overload and Its Effect on Focus

Minimizing Information Overload
- Organize Your Thoughts
- The 2-Minute Rule
- Similarity of Tasks
- Avoid Multitasking
- Limit Distractions
- Take Breaks

Chapter 7 – Memory Strength Training: What You Need to Know Create a Stronger Mind

Information Association
- The PNN

Universal Questions

Visualization
- What Is Visualization?
- The 5-Day Visualization Workout
- Movie Marathon

Grouping Related Information

Mnemonics
- Name Mnemonics
- Word or Expression Mnemonics
- Rhyming Mnemonics

Spaced Repetitions

Writing Things

Chapter 8 – Even More Mental Exercises For a Better, Stronger Mind

Meditation
- Quick Meditation

Drawing
- What Is a Mind Map?
- Why Do You Use Mind Maps?
- How to Make Mind Maps?
- Creating Mind Maps
- How Do Mind Maps Improve Memory?

Teaching Others

Pegword Method

Chapter 9 – The Movie in Your Mind

The Memory Palace

Mental Cues and How to Create Them

Chapter 10 – Strong Body, Strong Mind

Benefits of Exercise on the Mind
- Tips on Exercises to Keep the Brain Healthy

Sleep and Memory

Conclusion

References

YOUR FREE GIFT

Thank you for purchasing my book! To show my gratitude, I'd like to give you another companion book for FREE that's only available to the readers of my book.

17 Simple Strategies to Improve Your Memory includes even more memory tests, unique memory strategies, and even more tips and tricks to achieve your mental mastery goals.

Go to the URL below to get instant access:

http://mentalmasterymethods.com/remembermore

Introduction

Take one quick look at the arrangement of letters below, close your eyes and then try to recollect them in the order they are shown within a span of a few seconds:

KGBNSAUSSRUNESCOFBI

It is not so easy, is it? Not only does the arrangement of letters appear random, but our brains enter a state of stress because of the time limit. If our brains had the freedom of time, then perhaps they would be able to collate the letters more accurately.

Let's try the exercise again, but this time, we are going to split the letters into groups.

KGB NSA USSR UNESCO FBI

Try closing your eyes and recollecting the letters this time. You might find that it is much easier to do so. As soon as we arrange the letters in meaningful patterns, our brains recognize those meanings and are able to recall them better.

In 2016, neuroscientists discovered that the human brain's storage capacity was 10 times more than what was originally calculated a few years earlier. According to them, the human brain can store up to 1 petabyte, or 1,000,000 gigabytes, of information (Ghose, 2016). With such a staggering storage capacity, why does the brain fail to recollect a simple arrangement of letters?

Let's try and look at a scenario. You are at a party and meet some interesting people. One of them introduces himself and you realize that the person has made a positive impression on you. He might be someone you won't forget about easily. Yet the next day, when you try to remember his name, you realize your brain draws a blank. Try as you might to focus, you cannot conjure the name of the person. You are hoping that the name explodes into your mind, like fireworks in the night sky. But nothing seems to happen.

Think of other situations in your life where your memory deserts you when you need it the most. You forget phone numbers. You can't seem to remember where you put the car keys—again. It is your spouse's/friend's/child's/family member's birthday and the only reason you became aware of it is because you checked Facebook. Now, you pretend you knew it all along and maybe even throw in a "I would never forget such a special day" when the person asks you if you had forgotten their birthday. Inwardly, you decide that next year you are going to be more vigilant.

You might have experienced such "brain fogs," moments where memories are either hazy or always feels like they are beyond your mental grasp, numerous times in your life. Brain fogs could either be a recurring problem or they could hinder your memory during certain moments in your life.

When we experience this brain fog, we often wonder if we are getting old, our memory is degrading, or if we truly don't have a good memory in the first place because of our genes (curse you, DNA!). Instead, we should be looking at our brains because, chances are, they might just be frazzled due to unhealthy habits, lack of stimulation, extreme stress, or information overload. Our brains have reached a brain-dead end.

But despite everything, our brains are constantly changing. It changes every day as you go through experiences. It is changing right now as you read the words on this page. This process of change is termed "brain plasticity," and it is the solution to our memory problems, if we can take advantage of it.

You see, we can help the brain form changes that are advantageous to the memory. Scientists studying these changes noticed them in a research conducted on taxi drivers and the hippocampus (Maguire, Woollett & Spiers, 2006).

The hippocampus is the part of the brain that helps with short-term and long-term memory, as well as spatial memory. Your spatial memory is what you use to navigate in the environment, whether in a particular area or within a structure, like a building or your home.

As taxi drivers spend more time on their job navigating the streets, alleys, and other locations of a city, their hippocampus grows in size. This growth helps the drivers develop their spatial memories even more, giving them the ability to recollect and visualize routes and locations with incredible levels of accuracy. If taxi drivers can do it, so can you. The only difference is that you are going to consciously practice improving your brain and through that, your memory.

This book is going to guide you through the process of memory training. You are going to understand how you can transform your memory from working at a snail's pace to running at faster speeds. You are going to strengthen your memory and learn techniques to store large pieces of information. Then you are going to improve your ability to recollect things.

But why should you listen to me? What makes me ideal to approach this subject?

My name is James Stephenson and I was frustrated with how inaccessible my memory was. I would forget phone numbers. When someone mentioned the name of a person, I was sometimes not able to connect the name to a face, even though I had met the person the previous day. In similar ways, I was unable to recollect simple information. This led me on a quest to bolster my memory and soon, I became passionate about understanding how to remember more, how they can learn things faster, and how the mind works.

The more I learnt, the more revelatory the information became. I began to accumulate a plethora of information about memory and practice numerous memory techniques and exercises. And the more I continued to explore the intricacies and details of our memory, the more I was compelled to share the knowledge I had gained with others.

I started working with people to implement the methods I had discovered. I noticed the improvements, and when they began to thank me for changing their lives, I was compelled to compile the knowledge I had gained into this book to make the information more accessible.

As you practice the methods in the book, you should be able to retain information better and retrieve it quicker. Whether you intend to pass your exams, improve your performance at work, or impress people, this book will serve as your personal guide. You will become equipped with extensive knowledge about your memory and robust practical exercises to make a difference to your memory retention and recollection.

It is not merely for improving our memory that we should work on it. Let's take a look at another scenario to understand the next point.

Imagine that you are heading to the local store. You had a list of items that you wanted to purchase. However, as you are adding the items from the shelves to your shopping cart, you realize that you don't quite remember everything you should be getting. That's odd. It hasn't even been an hour since you made that mental list and you are already drawing blanks. You begin to wonder if Alzheimer's has decided to knock on your mental door early on in your life. But it's too early, isn't it? Although there are some cases of early onset Alzheimer's, you wonder if the condition strikes people who haven't yet reached their 40s or 50s (or even their 60s)!

While your reaction is understandable (and quite frankly, common), the odds are that you are not developing Alzheimer's. Your brain is simply experiencing a deterioration in memory assembly. Researchers have numerous theories that explain this breakdown, but the most prevalent theory is that as we age, there is a drop in the production of a neurotransmitter called acetylcholine in the brain (Hasselmo, 2006). This neurotransmitter plays a pivotal role in memory and learning.

Here's the kicker: Our brain experiences the deterioration when we are still in our 20s.

Now, this might alarm many people, but understand that it is a natural process. As we grow older, the neurons, or "brain cells" in common parlance, start breaking down. This should not be of concern because, 1) there are over 100 billion neurons in our brain and you are not going to lose them quickly as the deterioration process is slow and 2) the study of neurogenesis (which focuses on the production and development of the nervous system cells) shows that it is possible for neurons to be created in the brain (Underwood, 2019).

What should be of concern is the fact that we don't use the neurons we have to create connections. And that means you should be doing it now when you have more neurons in your brain than you will two years from now. You need to begin practicing the methods in this book today so you can strengthen your memory for the future.

The methods mentioned in this book can help people from all walks of life—from college students wanting that extra mental sharpness or grandparents wanting to keep their memory fresh. Each chapter in this book provides details or actionable steps to improve your memory.

With that in mind, let's take a trip down memory lane.

Chapter 1 - Welcome to Your Mind!

Did you know that scientific research has revealed that the human brain can form memories in the womb? Studies have shown that fetuses, at 30 weeks of age, are capable of creating short-term memories (Rettner, 2019).

That shows something incredible. The human mind is truly powerful. That's what makes it interesting to learn about...

...The Inner Workings of Your Mind

The mind is truly an exceptional machine. From an engineering standpoint, it is a model of effectiveness and efficiency. It is for this reason that scientists have spent years of research to understand what makes us "intelligent." It is still unclear just how the mind works. After all, it isn't a tangible entity that can be examined under a microscope or tested in lab conditions. Psychologists, philosophers, and scholars each have their own unique perspective about how the mind functions.

The most accurate answer we can receive is from cognitive scientists.

To understand the mind, we need to zoom into the cells in our brains and, most particularly, the neurons. The neurons are interconnected with structures known as synapses allowing information to pass between them. Together, the neurons and synapses form a complex network. Cognitive scientists believe that it is this network that forms the mind. Everything you are, imagine, like and dislike, and everything you know about the world is encoded in the synaptic network.

But aren't there other cells as well? What about their purpose?

The cells in our brains are broadly categorized into two groups. One group features the neurons, or the part of our brain that gives us the ability to wonder what plans to make for the weekend or wonder why is it that when we carefully choose the seats in a movie theatre, we are positioned behind supernaturally tall people while every other seat has a person with average proportions. Using our mind, we can truly focus on some of life's greatest mysteries.

The other group of cells is called glia, which refer to those cells that protect and support the neurons. In other words, any cell that is not a neuron is helping the neuron. Now, that's what I call royal treatment.

As we had understood earlier, there are about 100 billion neurons in our brain. With such a number, we are capable of making 1,000 trillion connections. In other words, this huge number: 1,000,000,000,000,000.

It's mind-boggling (no pun intended) when one thinks about the capabilities of the mind and just how much information it can actually store. But how does this complex network actually work?

To understand that, we need to take the example of lightbulbs. Imagine that you have several lightbulbs all connected by wires. The rule is that if one bulb lights up, then the surrounding ones do so as well, but with less intensity. You now switch on the bulb closest to the center of the arrangement. Immediately, you notice that the surrounding bulbs have lit up, but they are not as bright as the center bulb. These bulbs in turn light up other bulbs in their surroundings, which are even less intense. This creates a cascading effect, with the lightbulbs losing intensity as the effect expands from the center.

Eventually, you will reach a point where there is not enough power to light up any more bulbs. That is how a neural network functions as well. When we remember something or think of an idea, the neurons fire up, create a cascading effect where the synaptic connections get weaker the more it moves away from the point of origin. The only difference is that the neurons in our brain do not stay lit for a long time. They light up and then slowly start to fade. The entire process happens so quickly. Neurons light up for a period of just a few nanoseconds, enough for it to transfer the information and make connections.

As different neurons light up, different kinds of information is passed around in our brain. Anything from the way we behave in social settings to our favorite color or the fact that we don't like raisins in muffins are all the result of certain synapses activating.

All of this is important for the purpose of pattern recognition.

The Pattern of Predictions

Think about the act of cooking. You are about to start preparing something you haven't tried before. At first, you are rather clumsy, making mistakes with the measurements or the process. Over time, you begin to gain a level of mastery over the recipe until you can prepare it smoothly. You might even gain the ability to check what is wrong with the recipe by simply tasting it. This level of recognition of the dish and all its components is possible because of one crucial process: pattern recognition.

Now, think about this scenario. You wake up in the morning and head down to the kitchen. It's time for some coffee to kickstart your day! You pour in all the ingredients into the coffee maker and wait for it to prepare the drink. Soon, the aroma of coffee drifts over to you and you can barely wait to start sipping the drink.

It is at this moment that you realize something: You do not know where you have placed your favorite mug. You look around the kitchen, trying to dig deep into your memory to discover where you might have misplaced it. Eventually, you spot a familiar black mug handle behind a jar of cookies. You have no doubt that you are looking at the handle of your favorite mug. But how could you have guessed that you are looking at your mug by merely glimpsing the handle? How did the brain process the information to confirm your conclusion?

Once again, you are using the process of pattern recognition. Just like with the recipe, where you can easily recognize each component of the dish, you can easily recognize each component of your mug. This is because you have been using the mug repeatedly, allowing your brain to learn its details, texture, weight, and aesthetics. When you see only a part of the mug, your brain can fill in the missing details and form the full shape of the mug.

But that's not all. If we stop to think about it, then we can imagine ourselves lifting the mug. We can imagine how it looks with coffee inside it and even imagine ourselves drinking from that mug. By closing our eyes, we can create images about the mug.

In the above example, not only were we able to notice the partially hidden cup easily, but we could also form mental pictures about it. This is possible because of pattern recognition as well. Our brains are able to fully recreate the mug and is capable of imagining it in different situations and environments.

But our abilities of recognition and imagination won't matter if we didn't have one crucial ability: our memory.

What Is Memory?

Memory is the brain's ability to acquire, encode, and store information that can be recalled in the future.

In the 1960s, there was a period during when it was hypothesized that nearly all the cells in the body had the ability to store memories and that memory was not restricted to the brain alone. This idea was known as cellular memory, or cell memory for short, and it was developed based on two researches.

One was based on flatworms. These creatures were chosen for the experiment because they have a centralized brain, a structure that is also found in mammals. They also possess an incredible ability to regenerate themselves from small parts of flesh. For example, if you sever the tail of a flatworm, within a mere 2 weeks, the tail grows into a new specimen with a fully functioning brain. Researchers had also discovered that by using electric shocks, they could teach the flatworms certain behaviors. They could, for example, force the flatworms to move to a particular part of a petri dish.

At that time, a psychology professor at Michigan University, by the name of Dr. James V. McConnell, wanted to test a new theory he was working on. If he could demonstrate that a flatworm could recollect its behaviors after its head had been cut off and a new head had developed, then he would be able to conclude that the experiment was a sign that memories were stored outside the brain. McConnell had successfully conducted his experiment. However, when the experiment was replicated by many other scientists during that time, they failed to create the results that McConnell did and eventually, they rejected the cellular memory theory.

The other research of cellular memory was based on organ transplant patients. In 2006, a 63-year-old man underwent a heart transplant surgery. Prior to the surgery, the man had no artistic abilities, but after receiving the new heart, the man discovered that his artistic abilities had developed dramatically. It was then discovered that the heart donor was a talented artist. Could it be that the donor transferred his skills over to the recipient of the transplant?

Studies were then conducted on other organ transplant patients. In one study of 10 organ transplant recipients, it was discovered that each recipient had at least two to five parallels with their respective donor's behavior (Pearsall, Schwartz & Russek, 2000). However, when researchers studied many other organ donor cases, it was discovered that there were only a small number of cases where the recipient had developed personality changes. They suggest that drawing parallels does not prove any link because if one examines the lives of people, then parallels can be drawn between any two similar behaviors whose existence is pure coincidence. When asked about the behavioral changes of recipients, researchers explain that organ transplant is a traumatic and life-threatening procedure. Any behavioral changes resulting from the procedure is purely coincidental.

Let's take the example of the 63-year-old man. He might have developed newfound artistic abilities, but that does not mean he was incapable of painting before the organ transplant surgery. It just might be something that was never a priority to him. After the surgery, he forms a new appreciation for the talent and devotes his entire attention to art, which could explain why the man was able to create better works of art after the procedure; he was working on his art in earnest. If the donor had also possessed artistic abilities, then it does not mean that they passed on the talents to the recipient. The resulting behavior or abilities can be due to various psychological and emotional circumstances.

The strange aspect of the two theories mentioned above is that researchers have not debunked them entirely. Even McConnell's experiment was not entirely debunked, merely disputed. This is because the memory is a complex construct and studies are still conducted to fully understand it. What we do know is that memory is classified into various categories based on types and stages.

Based on Types

The memory is divided into explicit and implicit memory.

Explicit Memory

We can access our explicit memory easily because they represent the knowledge or information that can be consciously recollected. For example, when we forget the name of a song, we dive down deep into our memory reserves to discover the information we seek. We use the same process when we are entering a password or signing a document, since a signature represents our ability to remember a pattern. There is a conscious attempt to retrieve the memory we want.

Implicit Memory

Implicit memory consists of information of influences that we cannot consciously access. For example, when we spot an elderly person trying to cross the street, we decide to help the person because our subconscious mind brings our feelings of empathy. We understand, to the best of our capabilities, how difficult it is for elderly people to cross the street. We don't consciously create this feeling of empathy. Our mind conjures it because it is something we had learned in the past, perhaps because we were close to our grandparents or we knew someone who was old and had a major influence in our lives. This process, where a stimulus from the past affects the actions of the present, is called priming and is one of the ways our intrinsic memory becomes activated.

Based on Stages

When you categorize memory based on stages, then you have three divisions: sensory, short-term, and long-term divisions.

Sensory Memory

Your sensory memory stores sensory information for a brief period. It is a form of buffer that keeps information for you to deal with immediately. If the information is ignored, then it is purged and forgotten. On the other hand, if you attend to the information, then it gets processed for future use.

For example, imagine that you are walking home from work. Along the way, you pass many sights such as buildings, people, vehicles, and other objects. None of them hold any significance to you and for that reason, you dismiss the images you receive as soon as they enter your field of vision. Your sensory memory is constantly working, taking in the sights but dismissing them because they are irrelevant.

Now, imagine that you notice a strange sight. A clown is riding a unicycle while juggling three bowling pins. If that sight is fairly common in your city, then try this: A clown is pantomiming on the roof of a cab wearing a pirate hat and a disco outfit. And if that sight is still fairly common in your city, then you need to let me know where you live! But, let's proceed with the example. You notice this strange sight and your sensory memory is absorbing information about what you are seeing. Since you are interested in the sight, your sensory memory does not dismiss the information immediately. The information is passed on to the short-term memory for further processing.

Your sensory memory is further divided into two types. There is the iconic memory, which gets information from your visual sense, and the echoic memory, which is reliant on your auditory sense. Among the two, iconic memory lasts for around 250 milliseconds, or about a quarter of a second. In the clown example before, the reason you were able to dismiss all the irrelevant information from your memory so quickly was because they were held for such a miniscule period in your brain. Your echoic memory can hold on to a particular information for as long as four seconds. For example, when someone is dictating a statement to you, then you are able to write down the statement long after the person has finished speaking it.

A small percentage of the world's population have an enhanced iconic memory, where the information is stored longer. This phenomenon is known as eidetic memory. You might be aware of it by its other name, photographic memory. Most of the people who possess eidetic memories also have psychological disorders such as autism. But eidetic memory is almost like a superpower, since people can recollect images long after they have seen them with near-perfect clarity. It is no wonder that movies and works of fiction often depict eidetic memory as a unique skill of a particular character.

Short-Term Memory

Most of the information that passes through the sensory memory gets discarded. Don't believe me? Try this little experiment: Step outside and look from the left to your right, taking in as much information as possible. Now, close your eyes and try and recall everything that you just saw. Even if you decide to be more aware of your surroundings, chances are that you won't be able to recall everything you see. Open your eyes and examine your environment. Look at all the details that you had missed during your initial examination. You might find that your memory failed to store information about some or many objects in the environment.

But when we turn our attention to certain information in our sensory memory, that information gets passed on to the short-term memory, or STM. You can keep information in the short-term memory for longer than a few seconds and less than a minute. Any information in the STM is not stored for long and is made available to use so that we can modify, make sense of, store or interpret it. This information is also known as the working memory.

Although we use the term "working memory," we are not actually referring to a memory, but to a set of operations or procedures. We work on the information that we have in our short-term memory the way a computer works on a command; it takes in the information, reads it, analyzes it, and then executes it. Because STM does not hold information for too long, it cannot store huge amounts of data. According to George Miller, who was one of the founders of cognitive neuroscience and cognitive psychology, people can hold anywhere from 5 to 9 bits of information. He mentioned that most people can store an average of 7 pieces of information.

But that isn't right. How about the fact that some people can remember phone numbers that are 10 digits long or complex passwords?

The ability for our brains to recollect longer pieces of information comes down to a process called "chunking," where we, or our brain, group together the information we receive. This means that rather than looking at a phone number as 10 digits long, our brain groups some of the numbers and brings it down to a manageable 9 or fewer bits of information. By grouping information, we can also learn things better. For example, when we are reading a long sentence, the best way to commit it to memory is by chunking the sentence into meaningful bits.

Any information that successfully moves past the STM may enter our long-term memory.

Long-Term Memory

Earlier, we had seen that the memory capacity of our brains was about 1 petabyte. Theoretically, the storage capacity of our brains could be practically limitless. This is because no one can accurately pinpoint just how much information our brains can store. Everything that we know about our long-term memory's capacity is based on theories.

Information stored in our long-term memory vaults may last for a few minutes or a lifetime. The main sources of information in long-term memory (LTM) are semantics (information based on meaning) and visual (information based on images). However, even acoustics (information based on sounds) and odors (information based on smells) can be stored in our long-term memory.

Your long-term memory is further divided into many types. The first is the procedural memory, which is responsible for remembering how to do things or, in other words, it is your motor skills memory. You do not involve your conscious when using your procedural memory. For example, when you drive your car or ride your bicycle, you are using your procedural memory.

The second is your semantic memory, which is used to store information about the environment and the world in general. The knowledge you have about language, meaning of words, the capitals of cities, and other such information are handled by your semantic memory. Information in the semantic memory is declarative. This means that we know that something is what it is. The sun is hot, the air is transparent, and Moscow is the capital of Russia are some examples of declarative statements that semantic memory stores.

Finally, episodic memory stores information about various events that we experience in our lives. Episodic memory allows us to recollect certain incidents that had an impact in our lives, such as our first day at work or the day we proposed to our partner.

Now that we have understood how memory works and the different types of those memories, let's look at the process of memory.

Memory Process

Your memory is created and processed using three steps: encoding, storage, and then the retrieval.

Encoding

Encoding is the first step taken by your brain to create a memory. Your brain does not encode a memory unless it holds some significance to you. For example, imagine that you have traveled to an exotic location for the first time. You are truly blown away by the incredible vistas and experiences you had while on the trip. Once you return home, you cannot explain the incredible feelings and emotions you had gone through. All of your experiences, from the sounds of the waves crashing against the beautiful beach you had visited, or the smell of delicious food infused with various spices are all encoded by your brain. And it does this because the experience has left a distinct mark in your mind.

Your memory works the same way when it comes to other experiences as well. Think about the wonderful book you read or your favorite song. All of these sensory inputs are analyzed by your brain and transferred to your long-term memory if they are worth remembering. The information is then stored in various parts of the brain. When the time comes for you to recollect the information, the scattered bits are all collected together and made available for you.

Despite the fact that memories start with perception, the encoding process is carried out using chemical and electrical signals. Your neurons are connected to each other using synapses. These synapses transmit electrical pulses from one neuron to another, which eventually encodes the memory for you.

The connections created between various brain cells don't follow a certain rule or principle. People who go through the same experience do not share the same connections between their neurons. In fact, your neurons are constantly shifting and changing.

Your brain cells function cohesively, like a network. They arrange themselves into groups that deal with different information. For example, the memory of your favorite drink is managed by a certain group of brain cells while the memory of the incredible birthday you had last year is processed by another group.

At this point, we arrive at the concept of brain plasticity, or the ability of the brain to rewire its physical structure, similar to what we saw happen with taxi drivers as we explored their brains earlier. When a brain cell sends electrical impulses or signals to another cell, the process strengthens the synapses between them. The more signals transferred between them, the stronger the synapse or connection they have, which eventually changes the structure of your brain.

Storage

Once the memory has been encoded, it then gets stored in our brain. Most of the memories that get stored lie beyond our awareness. What this means is that we are not always consciously aware of them. These memories enter our consciousness when a certain stimuli or incident triggers them or when we find the need to use them.

Not all the memories that are encoded are automatically transferred to your long-term memory. Sometimes, even important information gets transferred to the short-term memory because your brain either deems it insignificant or it is the cause of stress. Your brain does not like to deal with stress. Similar to how your immune system reacts to illness.

Alternatively, you could also fail to store information in your long-term memory because the encoding process was interrupted. For example, let's say that you are reading this book and you are completely engrossed. Suddenly, the ringing of your phone interrupts your reading and you put down the book to answer the call. The interruption caused by the phone disrupts the encoding process and what you read might not be stored in your long-term memory. But that does not mean that once you have lost the opportunity to store information into your long-term memory, it is lost forever. There are ways to make sure you are able to keep the information, as we will see in later chapters.

Retrieval

When you want to remember a certain piece of information, then your brain performs the retrieval process unconsciously. You are never really aware of the steps taken by your brain to retrieve the information. You just know that when you want the information, it is available to you.

Many people think that they have a "bad" memory. But the reality is that people are good at remembering some things and are poor at remembering others. You could be great at looking at a painting and being able to visualize it later with impressive clarity, but poor at remembering numbers and equations, even though you have gone through them a dozen times!

But what makes someone poor at recollecting something? There are a lot of reasons.

Let's take an example. Imagine that you have placed your sunglasses in your bag rather than in their usual spot on your bedside table. You do not make a note of the change. It could be because the change is so insignificant that you might not bother thinking about it. You'll remember it when the time comes. It's in your bag, after all! Or it could be that you are distracted by other thoughts. Due to some reason, you did not pay attention to the fact that you have placed your sunglasses in your bag. The next morning, you are in a state of panic. Why can't you remember where you put those darn sunglasses?

The cause of your forgetfulness is because of one of several reasons:

- You did not clearly register where you put your sunglasses.
- You may not have made it a point to

retain the information about your sunglasses.
- You are unable to retrieve the memory accurately.

This is why, in order to remember something properly, all three stages of your memory process must be used properly.

Now that we know that our memory is capable of forgetting things quite easily, we begin to ponder about an important question.

Can We Really Enhance Our Memory?

Absolutely!

Think about the skills used by memory athletes. You might have seen them perform incredible feats of the mind, like remembering a really long sequence of numbers or attaching names to faces in the least amount of time. One wonders if these people are born with such abilities because no way can anyone achieve that heightened level of memory, right?

Wrong. In reality, most memory athletes are not born with any innate skills. Just like a golfer hits hundreds of balls or a professional swimmer swims numerous laps every day, a memory athlete simply works on his or her memory regularly, honing it to store and recollect large pieces of information easily. So, no—memory athletes don't possess strong memory capacities from birth.

In one study, non-athletes were given six weeks of memory training. What the researchers discovered after those six weeks was surprising. Not only had the memories of the regular folks improved considerably, but they were also able to perform the same memory feats that memory athletes were capable of. This study is remarkable because it shows that attaining a powerful memory is within anyone's grasp, provided they train themselves.

And you can work on your memory to hone it like a memory athlete as well. But before we begin to work on our brain, it is time to understand the basics of the human memory.

Chapter 2: Memory Basics that Everyone Needs to Know to Before Brain Training

Your memory is in fairly good shape. You do face certain "memory hiccups" many times in your life, but they do not always spell trouble to your memory. However, you are never fully aware of your memory's true potential. Those who put their memory to the test, such as memory athletes, are able to pull back the curtain on the memory's capabilities.

Let's try and give a score to your memory using a few simple tests. Before we start with the tests, make sure that you are in an environment conducive to learning. How can you make sure you are in such an environment? Try and find a relatively quiet place or at least one where you won't be interrupted by the cacophony of various sources. Once you are ready, you can begin the test.

Test #1

Give yourself a couple of minutes to study the words below. After the two minutes have passed, take out a sheet of paper and write down as many words as you can. Score 1 point for every word that you recall. Don't worry about the order of the words. What's important is that you remember each word and not the order that it is presented in.

TREE   TIME   FACE   PIPE

CLOCK   MOUSE   ENGINE   PLANET

THUNDER   NECKLACE   WARDROBE
CATERPILLAR

GARDEN   TREACLE   PICTURE
HARNESS

SLEEP   APPLE   OCEAN   BOOK

Test #2

Once again, take a couple of minutes to study the numbers below. Unlike the previous test, it is important that you remember the numbers in the order that they are presented. Take out a piece of paper or your notebook and write down the numbers, giving yourself one point for every correct entry you make.

In this test, you do not get second chances. Which means that if you entered five numbers in the correct sequence, but the sixth number happens to be wrong, then you get 5 points. You cannot count the numbers after the wrong digit, even if you have them written down in the right order.

Write down all 20 digits. If you find out that you don't remember the digits beyond a certain point, you can choose to stop, but be aware that you will be giving up your chances to score points.

5 4 0 9 2 0 3 5 7 6 7 6 7 4 8 2 0 1 2 9

Test #3

This test is similar to test #2 and the same rules apply. Take two minutes to study the binary digits below and then write them down in the correct order. Score one point for every right placement of number. Your test ends if you have guessed all digits in their right order or at the first wrong digit.

1 1 0 0 0 0 0 1 1 0 1 1 1 0 1 1 0 0 1 1
0 1 0 1 0 1 0 0 1 1

Points Tally

Once you have completed the three tests above, note down your points below. Then use the guide below to check your memory status. The maximum points that you can score is 70.

Score	Memory Status
55+	Expert
25+	Average
Below 25	Untrained

Here is what each of the memory statuses mean:

Expert

You have a strong memory, but that does not mean that you are a memory athlete. The above test was used to gauge how well your memory functions in a typical scenario. However, what you can take advantage of is the fact that you have a trained memory to use for the methods mentioned in this book. That could give you a little boost in improving your memory faster.

Average

You have great memory potential. All you need is a little bit of training to get there. Thankfully, you have in your hands the book that will help you work on your memory.

Untrained

Your memory might be slightly affected by your environment or situation. Keep in mind that an untrained memory is not tantamount to a poor memory. All it means is that when you have this memory status you have not had many opportunities to work on your memory. Think of the untrained memory as a body not molded by physical exercises; you cannot necessarily say that you have a terrible body. All you have to do is engage in physical activities to improve your physical conditions. The same goes for the brain with mental activities.

How Do You Train Your Memory?

As you will discover through the methods provided in this book, there is no single way to improve your memory. More importantly, you cannot only focus on the mind while ignoring the body. A healthy body contributes to a healthy mind.

We are going to look at numerous memory exercises and then move on to physical training as well. Don't worry, you won't have to necessarily lift weights, although a trip to the gym is always recommended.

As we run through various memory training techniques, you may come across certain words that might make you want to pull out your dictionary and check their meanings. But worry not, I have compiled some of the terms I think are important to know and understand when talking about memory.

The Basic Terms of Memory Processes

Stimuli

A stimulus is anything that causes a reaction or change in an individual's external or internal structure. The changes can be physical or mental. For example, when the surface of your skin comes into contact with something that is hot, then your brain perceives the presence of heat and signals you to be aware. Usually, you tend to withdraw your hand quickly to prevent the heat from causing damage or discomfort to your skin. Similarly, when sudden popping sounds cause you to jump, then you are reacting to a stimulus.

Neurological

This term comes from the word "neurology" and is used to refer to anything that relates to the functions, information, or study of the nervous system.

Synapses

Your synapses are the junctions between nerve cells. Many people might imagine them as bridges. But, in reality, they are actually minute gaps between one brain cell and another. As we have seen before, electrical signals pass between the neurons. If you have ever had the opportunity to see a plasma globe, then you might notice tendrils of electricity within the globe that look like electrical currents. As soon as you place a finger on the globe, you 20will notice a connection between your finger and the center of the globe. In a similar manner, tendrils of electricity exist between your neurons. The only difference between the globe and your brain is that the electricity you see in a plasma globe is actually the result of heated gas. In your brain, however, the signals are truly electrical.

Perception

Your perception is the reception, organization, and storage of information received through your senses. For example, when you are admiring the wonderful night sky, then you are using visual perception.

Recall

Recall refers to the act of bringing a memory to the mind. People usually use the term to indicate a conscious effort to remember something.

Engram

A change in the brain, usually permanent, that happens due to the presence of memory. If we return to the example of the taxi drivers, then the changes in their brains, particularly the hippocampus, was possible because of the presence of new memory. In similar ways, our brains go through their own unique changes based on the memory we focus on.

Active Processing

When a person actively manipulates or transforms the memory, especially short-term memory, then he or she is actively processing the memory.

Cognition

This is a mental process that acquires information, knowledge, or understanding through experiences, thoughts, and senses. For example, stepping out in winter without your jacket makes you feel cold. The realization that you feel cold when the temperature drops is a cognitive process.

What Elements Affect Your Memory?

The road to a good memory is paved with many challenges. You might come across certain elements that affect your ability to process memory.

Retention Ability

If you have been training your memory, then you won't have many problems retaining information. However, those who do not work on their memory may find it difficult to store and recollect information. Think of a bicycle that has been left outside for a long time without much use. A couple of years later, you decide to take out the bike for a ride only to discover that the drive chain is rusted. You have to first clean your bike and maybe perform some maintenance before it is road ready. Your memory needs constant stimulation if you want it to perform in peak condition. Otherwise, it might lose its ability to go through the steps in memory retention smoothly.

Good Health

A person with good health can retain information and memories better. When you are in good health, then important bodily functions, such as the transportation of oxygen to the brain to keep the brain sharp, are carried out without any problems. If your health deteriorates, then numerous functions in your body are affected.

Age

The younger you are, the better your memory processes. However, your age only indicates the efficiency of your memory storage and recollection capabilities at a particular point in time. It does not mean that you cannot train your memory to improve those capabilities.

Will to Remember

Your brain remembers because it wants to and discards any information that is inconsequential. But how does it decide what is important and what is not? Part of it has got to do with your willingness to retain information. If you show willingness, then your brain understands that you are interested in creating memories and pays more attention to the information it is dealing with. If your willingness to learn or understand isn't there, then your brain does not go the extra mental mile to retain information.

Meaningful Material

When you consider information as meaningful, then your brain considers them it important. This means that your brain improves its focus and memory encoding and storage capabilities. Similarly, when you want to recollect the memory, the task will be easier because it is meaningful to you and your brain recognizes that.

Proper Sleep

When you receive good sleep, then the connections in your brain improve. These connections are important to create better memories. The more neurons that are involved in forming your memory, the better chances you have of storing and recollecting that memory.

Why Do We Forget Things in the First Place?

When it comes to memory, things are never as simple as they seem. Consider the act of forgetting something. No matter how hard we try to hold on to a memory, we sometimes end up losing the information when we need it the most. But why exactly do we forget?

Here are four important reasons for our forgetfulness:

Failure in Retention

Have you ever been in a situation where you felt that a piece of information simply disappeared from your memory? Or perhaps the information is there, at "the back of your mind," as some people might phrase it, but you are unable to bring that memory to your conscious mind.

One theory that suggests the failure in retention is known as the decay theory. According to this theory, your brain creates traces of memory when a fresh piece of information enters your mind. This happens when neurons fire up and create connections within the brain. The theory suggests that over time, these traces begin to fade away and eventually disappear. If the information that is stored is not used repeatedly, then the brain slowly loses its grasp on that information.

However, in many cases, information is retained by long-term memory even if it is not recollected and used repeatedly. While the decay theory does explain why certain memories slip away from our minds, it doesn't mean that all the information that we store is eventually lost in time.

Interference

A theory known as the interference theory suggests that certain memories interfere with other memories. This happens because the conflicting memories are similar in nature.

There are two types of interference that can occur in the memory:

- Proactive interference occurs when an old memory seems to conflict with a new memory, making it difficult to store the new memory. For example, you have studied the subject of nuclear fusion for years. You could consider yourself an expert on the subject. Recently, a remarkable new theory has been developed that contradicts some of the older theories in nuclear fusion. You decide that you want to study this new theory in detail. However, you might find retaining the information of the new theory difficult because it has information similar to the old theory. Additionally, your brain has been holding on to the old information for some time now that it won't let go of the information easily.
- Retroactive interference happens when new information prevents you from

holding on to previously learned information. If you are trying to understand and memorize a complex topic, then you might have encountered times when you learn something new and realize that you can't quite remember what you had previously learned.

Storage Problems

Sometimes, the reason you have forgotten something is not because you cannot retrieve it, but because you had never stored it properly in the first place. When the encoding process itself is interrupted or improperly executed, then the memory is not stored properly in your long-term storage.

Think of those times when someone was giving you their phone number, but you were not giving them your full attention. Later, you realize that you can only recollect certain digits of the number. Was that a 0 at the end? Should I enter two 6s or two 9s? The numbers become jumbled in your mind because you did not take the time to properly commit the phone number to memory.

Intentional Forgetfulness

Sometimes, we make it a point to forget some memories or information, especially when they are uncomfortable, disturbing, or traumatic. When painful memories enter your mind, they can cause anxiety and stress. Which is why there is a desire to forget them entirely. When you intentionally try to forget something, then the process is known as motivated forgetting and it happens in two ways.

When you are using the method of suppression to forget something, then you are consciously trying to push the memory out of your mind. For example, watching a violent movie might store some of the disturbing imagery in your memory. At a later point in time, a certain stimulus might trigger the activation of those images. When that happens, you might try to forcibly forget those images.

Repression, on the other hand, is an unconscious method of pushing down memories into the depths of our subconscious. It is like locking away memories in a proverbial trunk and throwing away the key so that you do not accidentally open it and reveal the trauma that lies inside.

The problem with repressed memories is that they are difficult to study. Psychotherapists often use techniques like hypnosis to try and bring these memories to the forefront of the mind, but that only serves to understand what kind of memory it is, not how it functions. People who suffer from post-traumatic stress disorder often have repressed memories. The only indication that these memories even have an effect is in the habits of the people. For example, soldiers who return from war are often frightened of sudden noises because of traumatic experiences during the war.

The Power of the Human Memory

Despite the fact that there are numerous ways in which we can forget information, there are steps that we can take to ensure that those bits of information are retained well and, when needed, recollected properly. We need to give the brain what it loves so it performs better when it comes to memory tasks.

But what exactly does the brain love?

Chapter 3 – Understanding Your Mind: What Does Your Brain Really Love?

The term "brain waves" might conjure images of yoga, meditation, and talks about opening your chakras. However, the term has roots in scientific theories and explanations. So, what exactly are they?

The Different Types of Brain Waves

Your brain waves are a result of the electrical pulses transferred between neurons when they are communicating with each other. The best way to think of brain waves is to understand them as a stream of consciousness. If you place sensors on your scalp, then you might notice various intensities of brain waves and usually they range from slow and functional to quick and complex. Their degree of intensity is expressed in the form of frequencies.

One can use the analogy of music notes to best describe brain waves. When the waves are at low frequencies, then they resemble slow and rhythmic drumbeats. At higher frequencies, they are like high-pitched flutes. These frequencies are constantly fluctuating depending on the brain activity, our moods, emotions, and even situations. When the waves are slow, then we tend to feel sluggish, tired, or in a dream-like state, and when they are fast, we feel active and alert.

Having explained brain waves, you may be wondering if there are levels of activity that fit certain criteria. There are.

Infra-low: <.5Hz

Infra-low brain waves are called "slow cortical potentials." They are often considered as those frequencies that are the foundation for higher brain functions. Despite that, there is not a lot known about these frequencies. The lack of knowledge is because of the nature of these waves; they are so slow that they are difficult to detect. This also makes it harder for researchers to measure these frequencies.

Delta Waves: .5 to 3 Hz

Delta waves are slow like infra-low waves. However, since they are louder, they are easier to detect and study. They resemble a low frequency drum beat and are generated when a person enters a deep and dreamless sleep or during meditation. Delta waves are not concerned with external awareness and are considered to be the source of empathy.

Theta Waves: 3 to 8 Hz

These waves are mostly activated when you enter deep sleep, but you can create them during deep meditation as well. People who have experience with theta waves often claim that they lose awareness of the outside world and enter a state of inner reflection.

Scientifically, when a person daydreams or starts imagining, then he or she is using theta waves. You might have also experienced moments where you are walking home or driving along the highway and you suddenly have no recollection of the last five minutes of your journey. When that happens, you enter into a state of mild hypnosis assisted by theta waves.

Individuals who enter this state often remark about getting some good ideas. This is because, as we had seen earlier, theta waves help with imagination. The waves allow the brain to explore unique ideas and perspectives. When you are in a Theta state, you leave certain actions to the subconscious mind while you consciously engage with your mind, trying to solve problems or imagine thoughts.

In a theta state, ideation is possible because your thoughts are in free flow; they are not hindered by guilt or censorship. One might think that when thoughts are not restrained, they might venture into places that are uncomfortable or disturbing. However, the theta state is supported by a positive mental state.

Alpha Waves: 8 to 12 Hz

This frequency is often thought of as a state of rest for your brain, even though you are consciously aware of your surroundings and are not asleep. When you experience alpha waves, then your mind is focused on the environment. In other words, it is engaged with the present and aware of your surroundings.

But that does not mean the brain is resting. On the contrary, it seems like the brain is engaged more than usual. The reason it is considered as a resting state for the brain is because usually, your mind wanders, tracking thoughts and memories from the past or creating ideas and using imagination.

However, it is an active state. When your mind begins to focus on the present, it stops wandering too much and exists in only one place: the present. But since it lets go of various mental activities, it is considered to be "resting."

Your alpha waves aid calmness, mental coordination, learning, alertness.

Beta Waves: 12 to 38 Hz

When the brain is alert and actively engaged in creating memories or collecting information, then it generates beta waves. These waves are much faster than all the previous waves and indicate a mind that is working to accomplish something or get to a specific point. For example, when a person is conversing with someone, then he or she would be in a state of beta.

Gamma Waves: 38 to 42 Hz

These are the fastest waves in the brain, and when they are active, the brain is able to oversee multiple activities simultaneously. Gamma waves allow the brain to transfer information quickly between neurons. Initially, when these waves were discovered, researchers assumed that they were just extra noise from their instruments. Eventually, researchers realized that these waves represented a highly active brain.

Memory Preferences

While there are many people who enjoy reading a book, there are those who prefer an audiobook. They find listening to someone read the book out loud an easier way to digest the contents of the book and remember the words.

Some people can listen to a piece of music and then recreate it using an instrument. Wolfgang Amadeus Mozart is the best example of a person who could use auditory information and convert it to long-term memory.

Many people also enhance their sense of touch and are able to identify objects through physical contact. People who have lost their eyesight and use Braille alphabets have developed their fingertips to be sensitive to patterns on a particular surface.

The three examples above highlight different senses used to collect memory. Our brain is such as adaptive organ. It can use the power of senses to gather information from the surroundings. If the sight is not available, it can switch to our auditory sense. It is because of this adaptability that it is able to tap into any of the senses and use them to gather information from our surroundings and convert that information to a memory.

Our preference for gathering information from our senses depends on the situation and the comfort level of using the senses. For example, when we are listening to music, we use audio stimulations to record the memory of the song. When we are in a clothing store, we want to look and feel the article of clothing to see if it fits our preferences, using our visual and somatosensorial (touch) to capture the memory of our experience.

However, the question arises: Is there a sense that recalls memory better than the others? Turns out, there is.

If you had to arrange the senses based on how effectively they can trigger memories, then your sense of smell would be at the top. Based on memory recall, here is how the five senses would stack against each other.

- **Smell (olfactory sense, olfaction):** Certain scents can trigger vivid memories almost instantly. The smell of butter chicken can evoke memories of grandma's cooking or the odor of a particular perfume can remind you of someone.
- **Taste (Gustatory sense, gustation):**

Your taste is the second strongest sense when it comes to memory recall, which might come as a surprise to many because most people were expecting sight to make an appearance right about now. When you taste something, you can instantly name the flavor. Certain complex flavors make you think about how to describe them, but when you store information about a particular flavor, you can easily recall it.

- **Touch (somatosensory sense, somatosensorial):** People only think of your sense of touch as the one that is activated by using your hands. But your somatosensorial is much more complex than it. It is a broad term that involves the experience of being stroked or touched on the skin, feeling pain, and sensing temperatures.

Your somatosensorial sense also registers what's inside your body, which is important to know where your body parts are located in relation to the space and objects in the environment. For example, when you are sitting down, you know how your feet are positioned. This allows for you to stand up properly or adjust your position on the seat. If you did not have this information, you would be flopping around like a fish on land.

- **Sight (visual sense, vision):** Even though people consider the eyesight the most important sense, it does not fare well against the other senses in the memory recall department. Think about those times when you have looked at someone but could not remember the person's name or you spot a luxury vehicle you were reading about the other day, but its name has suddenly escaped your mind.
- **Sound (auditory sense, audition):** Think about this situation. You hear a song that you were so fond of during childhood, but you cannot recall its name. Try as you might, your memory can barely even conjure the first letter of the name of the song. The only option you have left is to type a part of the lyrics, or whatever you can remember after hearing the song recently, into the Google search bar and hope that it yields some results. This is a common occurrence for many people

because the sense of sound is the least reliable sense when it comes to triggering a memory.

In many cases, you do not use one specific sense to store a memory. For example, when you are trying out a delicious dish, you use both your olfactory and gustatory senses to store information about the flavors. Your senses also contribute toward the plasticity of the brain, where a certain sense develops in a certain region of the brain.

At this point, we have been seeing the terms "plasticity" and "neuroplasticity" turn up at numerous parts in the book. One wonders if they have any significance to the mind. Let's find out.

Neuroplasticity and How It Affects the Mind

Neuroplasticity refers to physiological changes in the brain that are formed due to our interactions with our environment.

When people compare our brains to computers, the comparison is partly true. Once you purchase your computer, you can automatically receive software updates. However, if you would like to change its hardware configurations, then you will have to do it separately. You cannot simply update your hardware through the click of a button.

Your brain, on the other hand, can receive both software and hardware updates through your interactions with the environment. As we have seen before, our brains can change shape based on the information and memories we collect in a process known as neuroplasticity. The important part about neuroplasticity is that it is not only important to biologists and neurologists, but psychologists as well.

Psychologists have spent a considerable amount of time, effort, and money to find ways to alter brain functions by modifying thought patterns. They aim to solve problems related to various psychological problems through permanent changes to the brain.

According to neuroplasticity, our brain is capable of making permanent changes to its structure. If that is indeed the case, then can the changes be used to solve mental health problems permanently? If a person is suffering from depression, then is there a way for that person to focus on specific activities that change a particular region of the brain, which eventually improves his or her mental health?

Due to neuroplasticity, the brain begins to form unique connections. These unique connections help the brain learn in unique ways. When you combine the connections formed with the physical changes the brain goes through during neuroplasticity, then you have a powerful combination.

Why?

Let's take the region of the amygdala. This region is responsible for memory, emotions, and survival instincts. Now, let's assume that you are using the methods in this book to improve your memory. As you begin to improve your memory, your amygdala also begins to develop. Eventually, the structure of your amygdala changes. It develops and so does its abilities. You find yourself able to remember better, your fight or flight instincts are sharpened, and you have better emotional strength.

The enhanced emotional strength comes into use when you experience negative emotions, such as anger, depression, or sadness. Your enhanced amygdala is able to deal with those negative emotions better and even generate positive emotions. By changing the structure of the brain, you are able to deal with your negative emotions more effectively.

In fact, in recent research conducted on the brain, it was discovered that people who suffer from depression have disruptions in their neuroplasticity (Liu et al., 2017). This research is quite revolutionary because it shows that the brain's plasticity is not indirectly connected to the effects of the mind, but directly related to it. The same research showed that hindrances in the plasticity of the hippocampus and prefrontal cortex of the regions increased the chances of depression in people.

The brain is interconnected in ways that researchers are still trying to understand. But what we know so far is that by improving certain aspects of the brain, we are not only causing physical changes, but mental and emotional ones as well. In short, improving the memory provides more benefits than merely granting you better capabilities to absorb and recall information. Which is why, we need to turn our attention towards memory geniuses.

In order to improve your memory, it is time to see how the experts do it.

Chapter 4 - The Mindset of a Memory Genius: What They Do and How They Do It

Here is the truth about memory athletes: They lose their keys too.

Nobody is perfect and the rule applies to memory geniuses as well. They are capable of making the mistakes that we do. But what sets them apart from the rest of us? How do they overcome the problems they face in their lives? What mindset do they have when they are focused on improving their memory?

The Mindset of Successful Memory Athletes

Train, Train, Train

The simplest solution, yet something people forget when they approach memory training methods, is that it all boils down to good ol' training. There are no shortcuts. You might have a pretty good memory already, which you might have found out after taking the memory test in Chapter 2. However, that can only get you so far. You still have to make the effort to bring your memory to the level of a genius. Memory athletes train using techniques such as mind palaces and mnemonics regularly until they are comfortable using the techniques without any problems.

Improve Your Goals

Build towards bigger mental goals incrementally. What this means is that if you get used to a technique, then start practicing another technique or increase the difficulty of the one you are working on. For example, let's say that you are practicing the technique of creating a mind palace where you have to imagine a particular space or location in your mind. You start off small, imagining your room or your house. Once you get comfortable using your house in your mind, move on to imagining your entire street or a bigger building. In such ways, make your progress more challenging because your brain loves a good challenge.

Surround Yourself with People Who Motivate You

Sometimes, you might have someone say that there is no point in improving your memory. After all, it's not like going to the gym where you can see visible results quite easily, is it?

Here's the truth: Do it for yourself. There are so many benefits to memory training, as we had seen earlier. Focus on the training you perform and the progress you make. Anything that serves to demotivate you should become background noise.

Try to be in the company of intelligent people. You will be motivated to learn and discover more. Both learning and discovery is important because it is memory training in action. When you learn something, your memory expands, and your brain learns to better store information. The more you learn, the better your brain becomes at information gathering.

Watch Your Diet

The research to find out the connection between poor diet and depression is an ongoing one, not because there isn't any evidence of a connection, but because there is so much more to discover. According to this research, having high sugar foods increases the chances of poor mental health (Sathyanarayana Rao, Asha, Ramesh & Jagannatha Rao, 2008).

But why is mental health suddenly the focus of this section? Aren't we supposed to talk about memory? Wait a minute! Is this self-help guide disguised as a memory improvement book? Not at all. Your mental health is important to understand because it affects your memory.

You see, when you have a poor diet, your mental health deteriorates, which causes your mental capabilities to plummet like a rock thrown from the top of the building. When this happens, you will struggle to focus on your memory tasks, since your mind is distracted by other concerns. Additionally, by showing the connection between poor diet and mental health, you get to understand how important it is to eat healthy, as it has both physical and mental consequences.

Change Is Not Instant

A baseball player swings his bat over and over again till he masters the batting skill. A fitness pro heads to the gym and keeps doing the same exercises repeatedly until he notices the change. A ballet dancer spins day after day till she masters the technique.

In each of the above examples, the person does not stop training. Even though he or she knows that the journey towards perfection is not going to be easy and, more importantly, not going to happen soon, they still keep practicing.

You should follow the same rule. Never give up easily. To stick to practicing, remember the below rules.

Rule #1: Keep Your Emotions in Check

Everyone feels the effects of frustration. From Michael Jordan to Ray Charles, people who have spent so much time on their craft go through periods of frustration, sadness, disappointment, anger, and many other negative emotions. Do not let the same thing happen to you. Be in control of your emotions. It is okay to feel negative emotions, but it is not okay to let them rule over you.

If you need a break, then go ahead and take it. Often, you might find that your memory seems to show no progress. But that is not because there are no changes happening in the brain. It is merely because your brain is getting adjusted to the new changes first. Think of the finger exercises that beginner guitarists perform to make their fingers flexible. After a while, you might think that the guitarists are not making any progress. But once they start learning guitar, you will notice the difference that those exercises made.

It is the same with your memory training. In the beginning, your training is going to be similar to the finger exercises used by guitarists. Eventually, when you start committing things to memory, you will notice the difference.

Rule #2: Practice Before Perfect

Reaching perfection is a good goal to have. But one does not reach there without putting in the effort. Keep training as much as possible. At the same time, make sure that you are not stressing yourself out too much.

Let's say that you have been practicing memory techniques for four days straight and on the fifth day, you had a long day at work. Upon returning home, you can think of nothing but heading to bed and calling it a day. At that moment, you realize that you have to practice your memory exercises.

The truth is that your mind is not in a state to accept new information. All you are going to end up doing is forcing your mind to focus and become even more frustrated because you cannot remember even the simplest exercise.

I am going to also recommend a relaxation technique further in this book that will help calm your mind. You can use that before practicing your memory techniques or anytime you feel that you just want your mind to settle down.

Rule #3: Don't Be Afraid of Challenges

If something becomes easy, crank up the challenge. Don't be afraid to face tougher challenges, as they help you improve your memory. Sometimes, the challenges are going to seem intimidating, but the trick is to not look at the problem and react to it. The trick is to look at the problem and *solve* it.

Imagine a chessboard. You are facing off against an opponent who is controlling black pieces. This means that you should make the first move. Once you have made your move, the opponent makes theirs and the game continues from there, each player getting just one move per turn. That is the beauty of chess and you can use the same logic to solve your problem: Solve one part at a time.

The Law of Averages

Motivational speaker Jim Rohn believes that we are the average of five of the closest people we have in our lives. His statement is similar to another idea where we can guess the future of a person based on his or her friends.

When you audit the people, a person is surrounded by, then you can get a glimpse of what the person aims to do with his or her life. This does not necessarily imply something negative. For example, successful people always surround themselves with other successful people. Those who are positive have friends and family who bring in more positivity.

Two scientists, Nicholas Christakis and James Fowler, decided to test the influence of social networks in our lives (Christakis & Fowler, 2011). They took data from the Framingham Heart Study, one of the most extensive and long-running health studies. The two scientists then contacted the participants of the study and asked them various questions about their lives, particularly in connection to obesity.

Ready to hear something rather mind boggling?

The results of the duo's analysis and research of the data and the interview of the participants yielded were:

- If an individual's friend becomes obese, then the individual is 45 percent more likely to start gaining weight.
- If the friend of the individual's friend is also obese, then the likelihood of the individual to gain weight increases by 20 percent. This happens even if the individual does not know the friend of their friend.

Let that sink in.

When you surround yourself with people who can motivate you, then you start noticing the difference in your life. Having like-minded people gives you ideas on how to improve your approach towards a problem, useful guides and research materials, and other important tools that are going to benefit you on your journey.

On your journey, you might discover some surprising facts about the memory itself, such as why it needs to forget in order to remember.

A Short message from the Author:

Hey there! Are you enjoying the book? I'd love to hear your thoughts!

Many readers do not know how hard reviews are to come by, and how much they help an author.

I would be incredibly thankful if you could take just 60 seconds to <u>write a brief review</u> on Amazon, even if it's just a few sentences!

Thank you for taking the time to share your thoughts!

Your review will genuinely make a difference for me and help gain exposure for my work.

Chapter 5 – Forgetting and Improving Memory

Do you remember the details of your first birthday? How about the dessert you had four weeks ago? You see, your brain deletes certain information or memories automatically and without your consent. While that might seem rather rude on the part of your brain, there is a reason for that.

Why Your Hippocampus Creates Memories and Erases Them

Oliver Hardt, a professor who studies memories at McGill University in Montreal, said that if we cannot forget, then we would not have any memory at all (Chawla, 2018). While that might seem like a rather bold statement, there is a reason for his choice of words.

According to Hardt, if we were capable of remembering everything, then we won't have accurate information and our memory system would become inefficient. He believes that our brains would be flooded with too many superfluous memories.

When we have too much information in our brains, then we end up having contradictory memories. Eventually, we might reach a point where we are sifting through our memories to figure out which is right, and which is wrong. Furthermore, our brains do not know which memory is important and which isn't. It constantly filters out old memories because it thinks that new memories are more important than the old ones.

In a study conducted on mice by neuroscientist Paul Frankland, the rodents were found to perform poorly on tasks that require them to retain information from the past. In order to make sure that the mice stored even more memories without deleting any old ones, their neuron birth rates were increased tremendously. This caused them to make even more connections without deleting any older connections.

The research was definitely eye-opening for many researchers since they believed that one of the effective ways to lower the levels of depression is to boost the neuron birth rates with antidepressants. Most researchers believed that increasing the neuron rates does not affect the patients in a negative way. That is, until Frankland's discovery.

The research gives us a glimpse into the machinations of our memory and why it is that we need to expunge old memories in order to create new ones. Our brains do not like to hold redundant memories since they only serve to confuse us.

Misidentification of Facts

In some cases, you brain might misidentify certain pieces of information as irrelevant even though you had considered them as important.

Let's take an example. Think about those times in your life when you decided to make a last-minute change to your plans. Maybe it was to attend a quick meeting with someone, drop by the local store on your way home, or maybe grab a sandwich for takeaway as you pass by a cafe. We completely forget to do the task and, much later, we realize what we had forgotten and react with a sense of frustration. The party responsible for deleting that information from your mind is your brain.

If you had all the information about your day stored in your mind, then chances are that you won't perform efficiently in other tasks. Let's take the quick meeting scenario as an example. Imagine that you have a busy day. There are numerous tasks for you to complete but despite the chaos of your work, you decide that you still have to schedule a quick meeting during the day.

Two things can happen at this point.

- You could become engrossed in your work and make sure that you perform your tasks to the best of your abilities. Because your attention is taken up by your tasks, your brain removes the memory of the quick meeting you had planned.

Or

- You could constantly keep thinking about the meeting and worry yourself senseless as you fumble your way from one task to another. Eventually, you have a streak of half-completed tasks and you know that your boss is not going to be happy about the results. But at least you are ready for that quick meeting!

Your brain is gauging your reactions towards various situations. When it realizes that you consider something important and that something else could possibly interrupt the important work that you are doing, it intentionally identifies the quick meeting situation is irrelevant and promptly removes it from your awareness.

However, that does not mean that you cannot make the brain remember the memory. If you really have to attend that quick meeting, then you need to convince your brain that it is absolutely important that you do not forget. One of the ways you can do this is by imagining what would happen if you do not attend the meeting. If the consequences of not attending the meeting can impact you negatively, then the brain understands the importance of the task.

The Decay Process

Transience. That's the word that describes the process of the degradation of a memory over time.

The way a memory is created is personal. For example, you and I could both go and have a cup of coffee at a cafe. We could even buy the same coffee. However, the way you record the memory is going to be different than the way I do it. To you, the flavor of the coffee might not be great. You might think about how the cafe chain's quality has been reducing in recent months. Perhaps it is only a matter of time before the chain starts closing some of its stores. I might be pondering about the weather as I sip the coffee. Perhaps it would rain that day, which would definitely dampen my plans (pun intended).

Why is it important to show that memories are personal? It is because of the personal nature of memories that our brains prioritize them. To me, the memory might be insignificant as I merely sipped the coffee and thought about the weather. To you, the idea that the coffee served at the cafe has a bad taste might be something you would like to share with your friends later on, perhaps to suggest to them to try another cafe.

When our brains deem a certain memory as irrelevant, it becomes harder to recall that memory in the future. Even if it gets transferred to the long-term memory, it begins to decay. The rate of decay depends on the irrelevance of the memory. For example, once you have relayed the information about the cafe to your friends, you might not need the information anymore. The brain allows the memory to decay faster. That way, it could make room for newer, and more relevant, information.

But it is not just the brain that contributes to the decay of our memories. Time is a proponent of memory decay as well. According to the trace decay theory, your brain lets go of certain memories because of the passage of time. As we grow older, we lose the ability to add memories quickly to our brains. This theory further suggests that in order to recall a memory, then you might need to follow a certain path or "trace."

A simple example would be those situations where you forget where you put a certain object. In order to find the object, you retrace your steps, hoping that a spark of memory might give you the answer. The more you rehearse the memory, which is the act of recalling it, the more you can delay the decaying process. If the trace is not used quickly after it is created, then the decaying process might be faster. For instance, when someone tells you their name and you forget it even though you had met them not five minutes earlier.

Distractions

A distraction can refer to any object or stimuli in the environment disrupts, distracts, or draws away our attention from a particular task in order to focus on another task temporarily. When you attend to the new task, then there is a risk that you might cause errors in one or both of the tasks. These errors are caused because your brain feels the stress of the distraction, which leads to cognitive fatigue. In other words, your brain become exhausted because it is dealing with two things at the same time and that causes stress. The stress forces the brain to shut down briefly, which causes memory lapses, mental slips where you lose focus of something, and mental omissions where you forget information you were aware of a few minutes ago.

When you are about to perform a task, you create an intention. The intention then becomes a cue for your brain to stop certain tasks in order to free up more attention. After that, you can begin working. When a distraction interrupts you, the brain has a new problem to pay attention to. It once again goes through the process of freeing up attention, thereby temporarily removing traces of the first task that you were working on.

When you were performing the first task, you were gathering information as you were completing the task. The same process happens with the second task, which in this case is the distraction. Your brain begins the information gathering process. However, you soon realize that the distraction is not worth your time. You return to the original task but your brain has to go through the information gathering process again, just so it can inform you about how you can continue your task. This way, not only do you lose focus on the first task, but you fail to gain any benefit from the distraction as well.

In some cases, disruptions can cause you to forget the original task completely. It is only after your brain is reintroduced to the intention or the cue that you become aware of what you had forgotten. For example, let's say that you received an email from your boss asking you to work on a project. The email you received from your boss is the cue. As you were completing the project, you notice your colleagues beckoning you as they stepped out for a break. The actions of your colleague is the distraction. You decide that a quick break might help you relax a bit. That quick break eventually turns into a long one and you return to the office having completely forgotten the task you were supposed to do. You sit in front of your computer and turn off your screensaver. At that point, you notice the email and it hits you—the project! If you hadn't come across the cue, which in this case is the email, then you would never have remembered to work on the project until it would be too late.

In a similar manner, any distractions that occur while you are practicing memory techniques will prevent your brain from fully absorbing the lesson. Your brain will not have developed further, and you will be left having to repeat the task all over again.

When working on your memory techniques, ensure that you are not distracted too much. If you feel like something needs your attention, then focus on the other task and make sure that you complete it before returning to your memory training. This way, you won't have to face the disappointment of leaving two tasks unfinished.

Chapter 6 – Information Overload

Try reading a book on quantum physics. Pretty soon, unless you are a physicist or someone who has studied quantum physics extensively, you will find yourself feeling overwhelmed by all the information you absorb. This feeling of being overwhelmed is caused by an information overload.

As technology improves, and we have access to knowledge and engagement at a click of a button, the amount of information we consume also increases. According to a study published by UC San Diego 10 years ago, the average American was consuming 34 gigabytes of information every day (Deleon, 2009). This was because, apart from cable TV, the internet was a place where interactions were increasing. At that time, Facebook and social media platforms weren't as popular as they are today.

Today, you might have your presence on numerous social platforms where you share ideas, media, and information. One common misconception about social platforms is that little information is consumed when going through these platforms. After all, we are just browsing, right?

Unfortunately, we are still consuming information, even if we think that all we are doing is simply scrolling through the platform. Every bit of feedback, comment, images, or any other piece of content is a piece of information. The more we consume them, the more our brain becomes overloaded with junk information. It is junk because the brain discards it quickly, clearing up space for more information. However, while you have the junk information in your memory, your brain cannot take in more important information. It has been overloaded.

Overload and Its Toll on Memory

Think about a jar of cookies. It is filled to the brim with cookies that are crumbled or have flavors you do not like. Imagine that you decide to bake some cookies. You learn the recipe and create it to the best of your abilities. You notice that the cookies have come out splendidly. You decide to store them in the cookie jar, but alas, it's full of those other, gross cookies.

Think of the jar as your brain and the unwanted cookies as all the unnecessary information that has overloaded your brain. The new batch of cookies represent the new and important memories that you would like to store.

Unfortunately, your brain is currently filled with thoughts. So, its main priority is organizing them well and checking each one to gauge its importance. This is why some people often get headaches when they are thinking too much. Their brain is actually busy sorting through the information that it has already received. Because of the amount of information it has to deal with at a single time, it begins to hit its maximum capacity and you feel the effects of that limit.

Let's take the cookie jar example again. Usually, you would empty the contents of the jar entirely and then fill it up with the new batch of cookies. You wouldn't pick each and every crumb and piece, check to see if it's good or not, and put it aside. It is much more efficient to clear the contents of the jar instantly.

Your brain thinks so too when it comes to the information it holds. Sometimes, when it realizes that you would like to store more information, it dumps the current information it holds quickly. In that process, it might get rid of certain memories from the past or memories that are important to you, and that's not a good way to learn.

Overload and Its Effect on Focus

Open a heavy metal track on YouTube and blast it on full volume. Now try writing a 2,000-word children's fantasy story about a happy dragon.

It's not going to be easy, is it?

When your brain has too many memories, they vie for attention. They are like the heavy metal track blasting out of the speakers: too loud for the brain to ignore. You are the happy dragon that the brain wants to pay attention to. After all, it is based on your cues that your brain can decide whether to absorb a new piece of information or not.

Your brain is also losing focus on other things as well, such as the problem you are dealing with or the project you are working on. You begin to notice that often you are absent minded or lost. Your brain also looks for other ways to tell you to calm down and give it a break. It makes you feel more tired than usual. You start to feel sluggish and might chalk it up to the long day you had at work.

Think about this situation. You have had a stressful day at work. The only thing you can think of is heading home and "hitting the sack." There is no way you can take in any more information. Soon, you arrive at home and prepare dinner. You decide that you are going to watch TV while having your meal. As you are flipping through the channels, you suddenly spot an interesting movie. You forget all about your tiredness as you become engrossed in your movie. Eventually, it's past midnight and if you can make it to the bedroom now, you can catch at least 6 hours of sleep.

When you began to watch TV, your brain was distracted from its mind-numbing task of arranging the information it had collected during the day. You are shifting its focus to something that is enjoyable, fun, and does not require you to think too much.

When your brain notices something interesting, it forgets that it is tired. It does not want to handle the overload of information. This is the main purpose of meditation as well. You force the brain to stop focusing on stressful tasks and simply bring its attention to the present. Watching a movie, listening to music, or meditating all serve the same purpose with varying degree of effectiveness: shifting the focus of the brain. You might notice that after you have shifted its focus, you are able to retain information better.

When you feel that your brain is overloaded with information, then do not force it to participate in memory exercises. This might add even more stress to it. Rather, try and meditate to ease your brain into a more relaxed state. When you feel that you are capable of learning, you can try the memory methods.

Minimizing Information Overload

Considering the fact that there is so much information surrounding us, from the sights, smells, and sounds of everyday life to the knowledge, interactions, and the work we take part in, there is no way you can completely avoid overloading your brain. Unless you decide to live in the woods, away from civilization. But since becoming Tarzan or Jane isn't in our future plans, let's look at some other ways to minimize information overload.

Organize Your Thoughts

When you find your brain filled with thoughts, then take out a piece of paper and write down those thoughts. Try and list as many as you can. You might find out that some of those thoughts have escaped your mind, but don't go chasing after them. You can always add more entries to the list that you are creating.

Now, prioritize the thoughts on the list in the order of their importance. "You need to have a tub of ice cream" obviously goes after "get that pending task done." Make sure that you are arranging them comfortably, where you are not stuffing too many tasks at one time.

As you are writing the list, you might notice random thoughts enter your mind. Make a note of them as well and give them importance. Once you have completed your list, do not think of any of the items on the list except the first one. Rather than letting your brain become a scheduler, which will only serve to stress it, you are dumping your thoughts onto paper. Your brain is now free to focus on other tasks.

The 2-Minute Rule

Become proactive in your life to minimize stress. If you have a task that requires only 2 minutes for completion, try not to postpone it.

Finish it immediately so that it does not pile up with more work later on.

Additionally, if you have a series of quick tasks, then allot yourself a comfortable time, such as an hour, to go through all of them. The act of completing tasks not only motivates you, but you feel a physical sense of unburdening yourself.

Similarity of Tasks

When you have two or more similar tasks, then bring them together. Let's say that you have to cook dinner and you notice that there are still dishes to be done. Rather than prepare dinner, have it, and then move on to the dishes, why not get your dishes done as you prepare your dinner? When you are able to group tasks, you can free up more space and reduce the workload you have.

But, how is finishing more tasks related to information overload?

Each task comes with its own set of rules, requirements, and goals. All of these factors are pieces of information that your brain handles.

When you have too many tasks, your brain has to focus on each task and its details and intricacies. The more tasks you complete, the less tasks the brain has to manage. So, why not finish as many tasks as soon as possible? Below are some tips on getting tasks done efficiently.

Avoid Multitasking

The problem with having too many things to work on is that your brain begins multitasking. You might have heard of people claiming that they are good at multitasking. But here's the reality of the situation: Multitasking is a myth.

"But wait, dear author," you say, "I can clearly listen to music and read at the same time. What do you say to that?"

Well, according to psychological theory (Napier, 2014), we are not actually multitasking. We are merely switching between tasks really fast that it feels as though we are multitasking. Whenever we go from listening to music to preparing that presentation to checking out some information, we are using a process known as stop/start. Your brain stops the previous task and skips to the next task, but you are not entirely aware of the process taking place.

Think you don't believe me? Then let's try an experiment.

Take out a piece of paper and draw two horizontal lines on it. Now, have someone time your actions for the next part of the experiment.

- Above the first line, enter this phrase: I am a great multitasker.
- Above the second line, write down this sequence of numbers: 1 2 3 4 5 6 7 8 9 10 11 12 13 14 15 16 17 18 19 20.

Check the time it took you to complete the task. It might have taken you no more than 30 seconds to finish the entire task, unless you chose to write a little slower.

Time to repeat the experiment. This time draw two horizontal lines on a piece of paper. Once again, have someone time your actions for the next part of the experiment.

- On the first line, write the first letter of the sentence: I am a great multitasker.
- On the second line, write down the first

number in the sequence: 1 2 3 4 5 6 7 8 9 10 11 12 13 14 15 16 17 18 19 20.
- Then go back to the first line and write the second letter of the sentence. Head back to the second line and write down the second number in the sequence. This way alternates between the first and second line until you finish writing all the letters and all the numbers in the sequence.

Check the time it took for you to complete the task, which might have doubled as compared to the time it took for you to complete the first task. This experiment shows that you cannot actually manage two tasks simultaneously. The same case applies when you are seemingly comfortable overseeing two tasks and you think that you are probably multitasking. Turns out, you are not.

Limit Distractions

Each distraction that you face is another bit of information added to your brain. But how can you avoid distractions entirely?

You can't. But you can minimize the number of distractions that you face while you are performing your task. For example, if you feel tempted to watch TV because you are in the living room, then shift to a different location within your house. If you think that you are distracted by social media updates, then keep your mobile devices and computer away from you. The more you encourage the distractions to control you, the more power they have over your mind. Eventually, you will be flipping through your Facebook feed without even having realized that you had picked up your phone to do it.

Take Breaks

By simply taking a 15-minute break every couple of hours, you can increase your efficiency considerably. Whenever you take a break, you are giving your brain the chance to hit the reset button. Additionally, you are not overloading your brain with too much information, which allows it to organize everything it has learned in the past two hours smoothly. Once it has arranged or discarded the information, it becomes ready to accept new information.

There are many ways you can take a break: meditate, listen to relaxing music, take a nap, or walk around. Ensure that you are not browsing the internet, reading a book, or looking through your social accounts. The point of a break is to reduce information addition.

Now that you know how to prevent information overload, it is time to examine methods that are going to strengthen your mind.

Chapter 7 – Memory Strength Training: What You Need to Know Create a Stronger Mind

In this chapter, you are going to work on some popular methods to improve your memory. You don't have to try the methods at first. Feel free to go through the methods and pick one that you think you would like to start with. However, once you have finished one method, move on to another until you have worked with all the methods.

Information Association

Earlier, we saw how the visual sense discards most of the information that it receives unless there is something unique about the information. Your brain functions in a similar way most of the time. You are more likely to remember a cup of coffee if you notice unique coffee art on it made by the barista than if it is just another regular coffee. This is because the brain is capable of getting used to information, stimuli, and ideas.

Your memory functions the same way. You might not remember every day you spend at your workplace. But you are more likely to remember the day your boss dressed up as Captain Jack Sparrow for Halloween. When something unique occurs in the environment, it breaks the monotony that your brain gets used to. Unique connections are formed in your brain and the memory becomes easier to recollect.

In the information association method, we are going to turn any piece of information into something unique. We are going to attach a colorful, vivid, or creative imagery for association with the information. To do this, we are going to use the PNN tactic.

The PNN

PNN is an acronym for Personal Nickname, a method that you can use to easily memorize words by creatively visualizing certain aspects about them.

When you come across a difficult name, you usually give it a short name, so it is much easier to remember and pronounce. The same principle applies here. What you are going to do is take a complex word and pronounce it slowly. This way, you should try and find another word or a group of words that are similar sounding than the original complex word. The new words we form create a mental image and become the nickname for the original word. And that is essentially the basis of the PNN method.

Now, let's get into the fun part!

Suppose that you would like to memorize the name of a country, like Switzerland. You use the PNN method and pronounce the word slowly. In this case, you break down the original name of the country to Switz-er-land.

All you must do is find similar sounding words to Switz-er-land (remember, be creative).

Here are some examples:

- Swiss Air Land
- Swish Her Hand
- Switch-her-land

- Spitzer Land

Now, some of the words above might get a chuckle out of you, but that is the whole point. You are creating a memorable aspect for a word. Every time you would like to think of the word Switzerland, you are going to imagine a Swiss Air flight landing or somebody's hand getting swished or even the Spitzer Space Telescope. The idea is to create a memorable mental image for the word that you are trying to remember.

It is not always necessary to make PNNs according to a similar sound of the given word. In fact, any other knowledge or related idea can serve as a nickname for that word. Let's take another country example. This time, we are going to work with Australia.

When you pronounce it slowly as Aus-tra-lia, it sounds almost similar to os-tri-ch. But sometimes, when someone hears "Australia," that someone might be reminded of a kangaroo. If that happens, then he or she can take "kangaroo" as the nickname for Australia.

Pretty simple, isn't it? This form of mental imagery works on a lot of things. For example, if you speak the word "India" and think of the Taj Mahal, then that becomes your PNN. The whole idea is to find something memorable to attribute to a particular word.

Use of PNN makes it possible to convert any abstract word, phrase, technical term, business jargon, difficult vocabulary, or foreign language word into a picture. So, you can visualize it and associate the related information with it easily.

Let's try and use it on complex words.

Take the word "excruciate" as an example. It means "subject to intense pain or mental stress." Now, we can read this word as "a screw she ate." To memorize this word, just imagine a lady who is in a lot of pain because of a screw she ate.

Another example is "transient," which means "short-lived or passing." We could break the word up as tran-si-ent or train-see-ant. So, you can imagine an ant crossing the railway track just when a train is about to pass. The train "sees" the ant just for a second and passes away. A rather outrageous bit of mentally imagery, isn't it?

One of the things that people notice is that the PNN tactic seems rather, let's say, comical, for lack of a better term. But that is the whole point of the technique. You see, the reason why your brain puts certain ideas and information into its long-term memory is because of the novelty of it.

The idea of learning new words is not something unique to the brain. We learn new words every day. However, it is how we learn those words that helps us remember them better. So, instead of finding novel situations to add words and ideas to our brain, we are simply using a shortcut to force a novel picture into the minds of our brains in relation to the word that we are trying to remember.

Universal Questions

This is an important technique to allow you to try and evaluate an idea, piece of information, or any other factor by trying to find answers in different ways.

The first thing that you must note is the six universal questions:

1. Who?

2. What?
3. When?
4. Where?
5. How?
6. Why?

The trick is simple. Take any idea or piece of information and then use the above questions to find more information about it.

Time for an example. This time, we are going to seek more information about the body taking in oxygen.

You first answer the question, "Who?" It seems like there is not a lot of answers for this one. Perhaps the "who" stands for us humans and all creatures on Earth who take in oxygen for survival. If you can make other connections for the "who," then go right ahead and do it.

Next, moving onto the question, 'What?' What exactly are we talking about here? It is the process of taking in oxygen. You can then ask the question, "What exactly does the process involve?" You will eventually find some pretty incredible information about the process of breathing in oxygen. In such ways, if you have any other "what" related questions that you would like to answer, simply add that in here and see what results you can get.

You go to the next question, which is, "When?" One query you can form using the "when" question is, "When does this process take place?" Your answer is probably going to be that it is during the act of breathing. As with the previous questions, think of other queries that you would like answered by using the "when" question.

As you move down the list of questions, you begin to form a clear picture of the original piece of information. You creatively used six questions to not only seek answers but teach your brain something new (which is like giving it brain food).

So, how does this technique help the brain remember better? It uses the benefits of information association to try and add more meaningful associations. By adding more knowledge, you gain a deeper understanding of the subject matter, which your brain recollects better.

Let's take an example here. You prepare your cereal every day in the same manner: You pour the cereal into the bowl followed by the milk. You have been doing that for years now and the routine isn't significant enough to remember. One morning, you try to add a little honey to the mix. This new action creates a unique connection in your brain related to the idea of making a bowl of cereal. In the same way, when you explore information in different ways, you add new connections to the same piece of information, and that makes it easier for your brain to store the information.

Visualization

What Is Visualization?

Understanding the term is rather complex, since there are so many sources that have their own definition of the term. For example, meditation and mindful exercises use their own understanding of visualization.

However, we can try and break down the process into three important points:

1. The main purpose of visualization is to communicate data. However, this data must come from something that is not exactly visible. It is a rather abstract process and cannot involve image processing or visual techniques (like photography).

   What this means is that you cannot look at an image and consider it visualizing. You can, however, look at the image and then try and recollect it in your mind. The difference is that in one step you are merely looking at the image while in the other, you are using the mind to create the visuals.

2. When you are visualizing, you can use the visual part of the process along with other sources like sounds and feelings. With numerous sources, you can add things and enable yourself to receive extra information.

3. Finally, the process of visualization can involve actions. This means that it does not necessarily have to be a still picture that you are imagining. You can think about something

taking place, like two objects interacting or something being created. It's entirely up to you.

So, we have gotten the basic rules out of the way. Let's get down to the actual process of visualization. The first process we are going to adopt is the 5-day visualization technique. Basically, set aside 5 or 10 minutes every day for 5 days a week to practice one of the below visualization exercises. I have even provided what visualization technique you should practice on what day, but feel free to switch them around to your liking.

The 5-Day Visualization Workout

Day #1

Look at a picture of your choice. You can even search for an image online if you like. Now, look at the picture intently for one minute. Your job at this point is to absorb as many details as possible. Next, close your eyes and then try to recreate the picture with as many details as possible. Do not refer to the picture again. Just try and see how detailed you can get the picture in your mind. Take 5 minutes for this process.

Day #2

Grab an object of your choice. I recommend choosing an object with fewer details so that you can start off with something easy in the beginning, but you are free to make it as challenging as you like. Observe the object and notice as many details as you like. Put the object away, close your eyes and take the next 5 minutes to imagine the object with as much detail as possible.

<u>Bonus points</u>: If you managed to imagine the object quickly (say, within 3 minutes), then you can take the remaining time to imagine the object in action. For example, you chose a pen as the item you would like to focus on. Once you have imagined it in detail, then try and imagine writing with the pen.

Day #3

This one is going to be a bit more challenging, depending on how many objects are present in your surroundings. Look around you at the room you are in. Try and observe as many details as possible. Then, close your eyes for 5 minutes and recreate the room in your mind.

<u>Bonus points</u>: When you get good at recreating the room, you can even imagine interacting with many objects in the room. For example, flipping on the light switch and imagining the light turning on. This technique adds a bit more challenge, but it flexes your mind more.

Day #4

In this method, you are going to observe the room you are in. Take in as many details as possible. Now, move around the room. Interact with objects and try out different activities. This time, try and imagine the smell of the room. Try cooking something and imagine how it might smell. Try playing your favorite music on your laptop or device and imagine hearing the tune. Essentially, you are going to use all your senses (touch, hear, smell, sight, and if possible, taste) in your imagination.

Day #5

Let this be the wildest imagination technique. In this method, you are going to once again recreate your room in your mind. Start off by moving around and interacting with various objects. Try to use all your senses. Now, imagine something completely outrageous. It could be a small dragon that flies around the room. It could be martial artists performing a complicated routine, an otter sitting on the sofa, characters from your favorite comic books or video games, or anything else that you would like to imagine. The idea is to make them as detailed as possible.

Movie Marathon

Why not make the visualization technique a bit more interesting? We all enjoy watching a movie or a documentary. Let's use them for your visualization.

This is an advanced form of visualization technique because it tries to store a lot of visual cues, especially since those visual cues are in constant motion. One of the things I like about this technique is that it is quite fun, since you can literally pick any movies, TV shows, cartoons, documentary, or even an advertisement for the purpose. The idea is to choose something that is available in video format.

The best way to explain this technique is by using an example. I personally enjoyed watching the *John Wick* movies, so I am going to pick that movie as an example. Ideally, I would recommend picking a movie that you haven't watched too many times as it adds a challenge to your visualization technique.

Once you are done picking the movie, follow the below steps:

1. Select your favorite part in the movie and watch about a minute of the sequence. We will be increasing the duration of watch-time later on, but for now, let's start slow.

2. Watch the clip carefully. You can only take one opportunity to watch it. No replays!

3. Once you have watched a minute of the clip, sit down, relax your mind, close your eyes, and replay the entire clip in your mind with as much detail as possible.

4. Once you have done that, watch the next minute of the movie and then try and replay that in your mind.

5. Do this one more time with the next minute. The idea behind not choosing the same minute is to make sure that your brain has a novel experience each time.

6. Usually, you will notice something interesting. The first minute that you watch will be the most challenging one. During the second attempt, the brain is reintroduced to the process. On the third attempt, the brain will be ready for the process and you will be able to remember the clip with even more clarity.

7. By doing this, you are training your brain to be more aware of what you see and your surroundings, eventually training your memory as well.

As mentioned before, you can choose any video for the purpose. Try this technique every day for 5 days. It will take about 10 minutes to complete the exercise. Note that you don't have to recall a clip perfectly. You just have to make sure that you are recalling as much details as possible.

After the first week, increase the view time to two minutes and then try recollecting it. Try mastering the 2-minute duration process. Do not increase the duration unless you are comfortable with a particular viewing time. For example, you can easily get used to recollecting a 2-minute sequence within a week. If you need more than a week to master recollecting a 5-minute duration clip, that is completely okay. You just have to keep at it until you feel comfortable.

Grouping Related Information

This process is also known as chunking. You take one big piece of information and then group it into small bits, usually bringing related information together. An example of this would be to try and remember this number: 4715856. Rather than read each number separate, you can group them like this: 471 58 56. So, you end up reading the number as "four seven one, fifty-eight, fifty-six." Trying to store phone numbers in such a manner, where you try and group the digits, makes the process more efficient.

In similar ways, you can use the chunking process on large pieces of information. Let's look at the piece of information below:

> There are plants that grow well during the summer, utilizing the abundant sunlight available. Then, there are plants that grow well during the winter, finding the cold weather more comfortable. Greenhouses help maintain a stable temperature within its facility, whether it is in the middle of the summer or during freezing winters.
>
> Plants that are subjected to abrupt changes in temperatures do not grow healthily. They are at a risk of losing their nutrients and even suffering from stunted growth. With greenhouses, you are providing a controlled environment for plants and herbs to not only grow but thrive. In

fact, you can even add specific features to your greenhouse, such as ventilation systems, to keep conditions just the way you, or your plants, like them. This becomes essential for growing certain types of crops, herbs, flowers, or plants.

Here is how you can use the chunking process for the information. From the two paragraphs, you have understood the below:

Group #1

Summer plants need more sunlight. Winter plants prefer the cold.

Group #2

Plants that face extreme changes in the temperature do not grow properly.

Group #3

Greenhouses help regulate temperature for plants in both summer and winter. They have a controlled environment and you can add additional features like ventilation systems to maintain conditions.

Mnemonics

Mnemonics are memory techniques that help you store large pieces of information easily. This works because you are able to make use of lists, including phases, parts, characters, and other associations. There are various types of mnemonics that can be used for various situations. Let's look at some of them.

Name Mnemonics

In this mnemonic, you use the first letter of each word to form a unique name, whether the name of a person or of a thing. For example, the colors of a rainbow are red, orange, yellow, green, blue, indigo, and violet. What's the best way to remember that fact? If you take the first letter of each word, then you get this word: ROYGBIV.

That does not make any sense. But if you turn that into a name, then you have something that you can easily remember. Hence, ROYGBIV becomes ROY G. BIV. That could be the name of a person, couldn't it? You can use this method to remember long lists. By converting the list into a name, it is easier to make information small and easy to recollect.

Word or Expression Mnemonics

This is the most common type of mnemonic used around the world. It is used to make either an expression or a word mnemonic by using the first letter of each item to form a phrase or a word.

For instance, in English, there are 7 coordinating conjunctions. These are: for, nor, but, or, and, yet, so. If you rearrange the words, then you get this: for, and, nor, but, or, yet, so. Now, take the first letter of each word and the resulting word is FANBOYS.

Another example that we can take is the order of math operations. They appear in the below order:

- Parentheses
- Exponents
- Multiply
- Divide

- Add
- Subtract

To help remember the order, we first take the first letter of each word. We get the word PEMDAS. We use those letters to form our mnemonic. For this example, the following sentence could be used: Please excuse my dear Aunt Sally. The sentence is quite odd, but that's what makes it easy to remember.

When creatures are arranged in the order of their categories, they form the below order:

- Kingdom
- Phylum
- Class
- Order
- Family
- Genus
- Species
- Variety

Take the first letter of each word and you can form the following mnemonic: Kings play cards on fairly good soft velvet.

Perhaps the most famous mnemonic is formed based on the arrangement of the 9 planets. They appear in the below order:

- Mercury

- Venus
- Earth
- Mars
- Jupiter
- Saturn
- Neptune

We are going to omit Pluto for now since the planet is going through a bit of a controversy concerning its status. In order to remember the planets, we can use this mnemonic: My very excellent mother just served us nachos.

Rhyming Mnemonics

When you want to remember certain instructions, then you can use rhymes. For example, I before E, except after C.

You can also use rhyming to understand certain facts. For example, the difference between cyanide and cyanate is that the former is a type of poison while the latter is a type of salt. Here is a rhyme to help you remember the difference: Cyanide, I died. Cyanate, I ate.

Spaced Repetitions

Earlier, we learned how information decays in our brain. We also found out that in order to keep it fresh, we need to rehearse the information or, in other words, repeat the information in our brains. Does that mean we should keep repeating until we remember? Not quite. You simply use a technique known as spaced repetition.

Oslo is the capital of Norway and Jakarta is the capital of Indonesia are facts that you might think are easy to remember at one glance. But if you don't recollect them frequently, then you might find yourself forgetting the statements later. This is because, unless you have been reading about Oslo and Jakarta, your brain will dump the information because it does not find it useful.

A similar phenomenon might also happen with languages. When someone moves to another country, picks up the local language, and does not speak the native tongue for a long time, then he or she might themselves unable to express themselves in their own language fluently. It might not happen immediately, but over time, the person might discover certain gaps when trying to express themselves in their native tongue.

You might have experienced such lapses in memory in numerous situations. Think back to those times in school when you were well-versed in a particular subject. If you try to recollect the lessons you learned back then, you will probably draw a blank or have hazy recollections. Your brain had been getting rid of the information over time as you entered your adulthood and absorbed more important information.

Spaced repetition considers the fact that time can cause information to go missing in the brain. It creates a repetition pattern to keep the information stored in your brain for a long time. Here is how you do it:

> 1. For the process to work properly, you need to have a box. The box should be divided into various sections, preferably 5 or more. Since we are beginning to learn this technique, let's use 5 compartments. Once you get used to the system,

you can increase the number of compartments. You can also choose to have 5 different boxes instead of dividing a single box into compartments.

2. Once you have chosen your preferred arrangement, number each of the compartments or boxes from 1 to 5.

3. Start creating flashcards for all the information you would like to learn. New information flashcards go in the first compartment because you would ideally like to go through them every day until you are confident you will remember them.

4. Information flashcards that you are slightly familiar with goes into the second compartment. You can read these every two or three days.

5. Information flashcards you are even more familiar with goes into the third compartment.

6. Following the above logic, fill up the remaining compartments with the

relevant information.

7. Using the schedule you have set for each compartment, go back to the information flashcards and rehearse them.

Let's suppose that you have memorized the information in the first compartment. How comfortable do you feel about your recollection of them? Based on your ability to recollect them, you can transfer them to either compartment 2 or compartment 3. Similarly, flashcards can also be shifted from compartments 2 and 3 to 4 and 5, based on how familiar you get with their contents.

The spaced repetition technique allows you to remember information thoroughly, even though there is so much to remember. The technique is also flexible because it gives you the freedom to arrange information based on your ability to recollect it.

Writing Things

Writing provides numerous benefits to our cognitive capabilities and helps us remember better. When you have studied something or mentally ingested a piece of information, you can then work on reinforcing that memory. You do this by writing down the information on a piece of paper.

But how exactly does writing benefit your memory?

When you write, your brain has to focus on the process of writing. Compared to reading, writing increases the brain's focus. When you write, you take advantage of your brain's increased focus. This means that not only are you repeating the information as you write, but your brain is so focused that it can store the information properly.

This double-reinforcement system of writing and focus allows you to encode and store information better. When you have completed two processes (encoding and storing) out of the three required to store your memory, then the third process (recollecting) becomes easier.

Here are a few writing tips that you can use:

- Take your time writing. When you write slowly, the brain slows down as well. This is similar to preparing a nice dinner, where you ensure that you follow the instructions carefully. You do not want to rush through the process, or you might end up making a mistake. Similarly, writing down slowly allows your brain to understand the information it is committing to memory without making too many mistakes.
- Have fun while you are writing! Remember how we learned earlier that the brain likes novelty? Try and doodle images or symbols as you write, whenever necessary. This adds more unique connections in your brain, and you may be able to recollect the information better because of the doodle. Additionally, you are giving your brain more ways to remember something.

Let's say that you are tasked with getting some items from the local store. You are supposed to get milk, some fruits, an assortment of herbs, and coffee. As you are heading out to the store, you hear someone say, "Don't forget the coffee! I might need it for tomorrow's dreadfully boring meeting!" When you reach the store, you forget the coffee, but because you remember the comment made about it, you immediately realize your mistake and make sure to buy coffee.

So, even if you happen to forget the information you are writing down, you might just remember the process of doodling, which will spark other related connections in your brain. It's like a road that branches off into different directions, but eventually reaches the same destination. If you find out that one direction is blocked, then you can use any one of the alternate roads available to you. In a similar manner, if some of the neural connections have decayed, the brain has other pathways to get to the information, simply because you created those connections.

Chapter 8 – Even More Mental Exercises For a Better, Stronger Mind

I have split the mental exercises into two chapters because I wanted you to start with the ones in Chapter 7 and get used to them before moving on to the exercises provided here. However, if you feel comfortable practicing many techniques simultaneously, then you can do so, since different techniques fit different purposes. For example, meditation is something you can practice anytime to calm your mind and allow your brain to settle down.

Meditation

Have you ever been in a situation where you are trying to think but unwanted thoughts keep flitting through your mind? One effective way to get rid of those thoughts and bring your mind to a calmer level is by using a popular meditation technique called Vipassana meditation. Here is how to perform it:

1. To begin, try to seek out a quiet place free of any distraction. These distractions could occur in the form of sound, smell, or temperature. Whatever environment you choose, make sure that it is comfortable for you.

2. Now, position yourself in a comfortable seating position. You can either choose to sit down or, if you find the opportunity to, lie down on a comfortable surface.

3. After discovering the ideal position, close your eyes entirely or choose to keep them open partially.

4. Once you are in a comfortable position, relax your body. Let go of the tension in your muscles.

5. Straighten your back and your neck. Pay attention to any part of your body that still feels restricted or tight. Relax those positions.

6. Start by focusing your mind on your abdomen. Focus on its upward movement, occurring when you inhale. Then, concentrate on its downward movement, happening when you exhale.

7. Mentally note the upward movement as rising and the downward movement as falling.

Do not speak the words 'rising' or 'falling' aloud. You are merely aiming to become aware of the process, not the movements. You will realize that you may not be able to keep your mind on these movements. You may find your thoughts wandering.

But remember, this is a learning process. Treat it as such. As with any method, you will slowly learn to master it. Once you have made a note of the rising and falling movements, you will understand that those movements are always there. You will have no difficulty in finding them should you lose focus during this meditation exercise.

8. Keep your breathing regular. Do not take in deep or rapid breaths. They might lead to fatigue.

9. Keep your awareness on the rising and falling of your abdomen while your breathing is calm and rhythmic.

While you are focusing on your abdominal movements, other thoughts will begin to wrestle for your attention. These thoughts or experiences will involve ideas, imaginations, desires, or intentions. Do not ignore them. When you imagine an experience, reflect on something, or feel like you must do something, acknowledge it.

Make a mental note of that thought. If it is an experience, note that you are experiencing. If it is an intention, note that you are intending. If it is an emotion, note that you are feeling. All these notes must be made mentally, without speaking aloud. You must note down each mental thought, feeling, or mental scenario.

When you find your thoughts moving away from the object of your focus, remember that you are wandering and bring yourself back to the original point of interest, which is your abdomen. Understand that these thoughts are simply a manifestation of external factors. Know that you are going to release them. Thus, after taking note of these thoughts, you are simply releasing the thought or experience from your mind. If you feel that releasing them is difficult, do not brush it away. Pay attention to the thought and its appearance until it passes away.

If you ever feel the urge to act, do it slowly while making a mental note of the action. For example, if you feel like swallowing, do so by making a note that you are swallowing. Similarly, make a note of any movement you make, such as straightening your neck or relaxing your arms. Once you have completed the action, return your focus to your abdominal movements.

When you notice the next thought or experience that goes through your mind, treat it the same way as you do with the other thoughts or experiences by mentally noting it and releasing it. Do not try to bring up any thoughts or memories by yourself. If you notice blank spots in your mind, continue focusing on the rising and falling of your abdomen. Allow your mind to rest during those empty moments.

Your thoughts might also appear as images. Once they occur in your mind, acknowledge them again as you did before and release them. If they do not leave, wait for them to pass.

Do not try to make sense of your thoughts. Many of them are disorganized and lack any obvious construct. You are only seeking to recognize them, not understand them. Observe them in a detached manner and release them or wait for them to leave your mind.

If you are a beginner in this exercise, you might find yourself struggling to maintain focus. But remember the steps and understand that you will gain mastery over time. You will gain a sense of openness and will learn to let go of the habit of evaluating or over-analyzing your thoughts.

If you find yourself reacting to your thoughts, wondering if they are good or bad, or if you should do something about them, make a note of your reactions. Once you have made the note, do not choose to react. Do not dwell too much on it.

If you still find it difficult to release a specific thought or image that has entered your mind, simply inhale deeply and exhale. While exhaling, picture the thought or image floating away with the breath. Once done, your mind is now ready to receive the next thought.

Should you feel uncomfortable in any way, such as an itching sensation, make a mental note of it. Be aware of the sensation until it disappears. If the itch persists, make a note that you are going to alleviate the feeling. Lift your hands slowly, focusing on the act of lifting and make a mental note of it. Reach out to the area and scratch it until you feel the sensation pass, noting that you are massaging. Return your hand to its original position, once again making a mental note of the action.

At your own pace, and when you are ready, observe the way you are feeling at the moment. Slowly, by keeping your breathing regular, open your eyes and take in your surroundings.

Quick Meditation

What if you were at work and you find out that your brain cannot add any more information to it? Your memory seems foggy and that task that your boss asked you to do?

Well, you have no idea what he or she was talking about!

Whether it's a busy day at work or you don't have time for a proper meditation session, you can use the below 10-minute meditation to calm your brain.

Simply find yourself a quiet spot. If you cannot find a quiet spot, don't worry. Just sit in an area where you will not be disturbed for the next 10 minutes. Turn off your mobile phone and any other distractions—you will not need them now.

Sit down in a comfortable position. If you think you would like to lie down, then find a comfortable surface for lying down. Adjust yourself if you feel you are not comfortable enough.

Now, take a slow, long breath and do the following:

1. Hold your breath for a few seconds and exhale in the form of a sigh.
2. Take another deep breath through your nose.

3. Fill up your lungs and your abdomen. Allow them to inflate as much as you can and exhale through your mouth with a sigh.

4. One last time. Take another deep breath through your nose.

5. Fill up your lungs and abdomen and exhale through your mouth.

6. Now, close your mouth and feel your tongue relax to the bottom of your mouth. Begin to breathe regularly. Do not take in deep or rapid breaths.

7. Simply breathe in a calm manner.

8. Now, bring your focus on each exhale.

As your mind focuses on the exhalations, you will feel more rooted in the present. If you encounter thoughts swimming in your consciousness, remember the Vipassana meditation. Simply note that you are getting distracted. Do not think about these thoughts further. Do not wonder if there are right or wrong. Their meaning does not matter. You are simply going to let them pass. Once you have made a note of the distraction and let it pass, return your focus to your breathing.

9. Continue to focus on your exhalation, noting that you are feeling grounded in the present.

10. Now, every time you exhale, feel each exhalation removing some of the stress out of you.

11. Continue to breathe normally. Inhale normally. Exhale and feel the stress melting away.

12. Now, turn your focus on your inhalations.

13. Feel each inhale enter your lungs and your abdomen, giving you a sense of peace and tranquility. Feel it bringing in positive emotions to your mind. Inhale your positive feeling, then exhale the stress away.

14. Finally, breathe normally and then return your focus to your surroundings.

15. Count to 10 and then open your eyes.

Drawing

We have learned about how doodling while you are writing can help boost your memory encoding process. Now we are going to enhance that process by drawing. The only difference here is that you are not only going to improve your memory but enhance your creativity as well. How are you going to do that?

What Is a Mind Map?

A mind map is a creative and effective means of note taking invented by author and educational consultant Tony Buzan. It is a graphical technique which offers an overview of a topic and complex information in a visual form, where we start with a central idea and expand outward to more in-depth sub-topics on different branches. Each branch holds a key image or keyword. Details are added to the main branches and radiate out.

Its structure is more of a radial type, like that of a tree seen from the top branching out in all directions from the trunk. Or it can be compared to a city map where different main roads starting from a central point of a city radiate in all directions, further branching into smaller roads and lanes spreading throughout the city like a web.

Mind maps have many applications in personal, family, educational, and business situations, including:

- Taking notes during a lecture or a business meeting.
- Summarizing a topic or a chapter you are studying for your exams.
- Making notes while reading.
- Mapping out your thoughts while planning an event.
- Setting career goals.
- Brainstorming various possibilities to work out a problem.

Why Do You Use Mind Maps?

Mind maps can be more effective than other brainstorming and linear note-taking methods for several reasons. A mind map can give you an overview of a large subject while also holding large amounts of information on a single page.

Instead of boring, linear note taking, the combinations of words and images with colors makes it more memorable and enjoyable to create and review.

It combines both left and right brain thinking, which means that you will remember the information better than if you just had lines of words. It mimics the way our brains think, bouncing ideas off each other. You can generate ideas very quickly with this technique and are encouraged to explore different creative pathways.

How to Make Mind Maps?

To draw a mind map, do the following:

1. Take a blank sheet of A4-sized paper. You can make use of any sized blank paper,
2. Turn your page on its side (landscape).

3. Start at the center with an image of the main subject (or main idea) using at least 3 colors. Starting in the center gives your brain freedom to spread out in all directions and to express yourself more freely and naturally.
4. Add the main branches representing the subject's main topics or themes using key words and images.
5. Add sub-branches to the main branches, having further detail with more key words and images.

A few things to keep in mind when making your mind map are:

- Make your branches curved rather than straight-lined.
- Use colors throughout and make your mind map as beautiful as possible.
- Write your words clearly in print and use only one word per line.
- Use arrows to connect linking ideas.

Your brain works by association. It likes to link two or three things together. Linking the branches will help you make connections and understand and remember a lot more easily.

Creating Mind Maps

So, let's try and put everything into practice and see if we can use mind maps for real life situations. We can start by taking a simple example. For this example, you are planning a party.

Let's say you have to plan your son's birthday party. A little planning goes a long way towards making things run more smoothly and in an organized way without any last-minute hassles. At the same time, you won't forget important parts of the birthday at the wrong time.

Mind mapping helps you plan by seeing the whole picture with all the good and bad possibilities. Here is a mind map presenting some of the possibilities and options. You can map out your own perfect party.

Step-by-step mind mapping your party:

1. Draw a central image on a blank page (a circle or a sideways oval, like an egg lying down), representing your party. You can make it stick in your memory more by drawing a

cake or a balloon on it (make it creative).

2. Draw your big main branches coming off this image. These branches may give you answers to the following:

   - When to have the party?
   - Where to have it?
   - Who will be invited?
   - Theme of the party
   - Food
   - Music
   - Games
   - Gift bags

Draw each branch in a different color to make it stand out. For example, the branch for "When to have the party?" might be green, the "Where to have it?" branch could be red, and so on. However, don't sweat it if you do not have different colors. You can use a single color for the purpose. It won't affect the overall result, just the aesthetics. The most important thing to do is to name the branches so you know which branch is focused on what topic.

3. Once you have the main branches, you can add sub-branches by adding

further details and options to the main branch. For example, while thinking of where to have the party, you can have options like whether to have it at home, a nearby club, or a restaurant. This way, the club becomes one sub-branch, the restaurant becomes another, and so on.

4. Repeat the above step with all the other branches.

You can keep on adding extra branches and putting in as much detail as you like. For example, we currently have eight main branches. But you might want to add other important factors that you would like to consider, like transportation, time of day, afterparty event, among others. You will be amazed by the number of ideas coming out of your mind that otherwise you might not have thought you'd have had you not been using a mind map.

After looking at all the possibilities, you can choose the best options according to your time, budget, and comfort. You can further plan what work you will do and what work you will delegate to your spouse, friend, etc.

Similarly, mind maps can be used to give presentations, in brainstorming the possibilities of increasing the productivity or efficiency of a company, in summarizing the points of a meeting, etc.

Let's take another example. This time, you are planning a trip and you want to make sure everything is in order. Usually, when we have to go for a trip, we make a list of all the things, to be carried and check with it while packing our luggage. Let's say you have to prepare for a trip to another country for a workshop.

- Below is the list of items given that you might need to pack:
    - Visa
    - Passport
    - Books
    - Pen drive
    - Suits
    - Towel
    - Band-aids
    - Cash
    - Organizer address
    - Tickets
    - Shawl
    - Gifts
    - Toothbrush

- Soaps
- Credit card
- Cold cream (if you need it)
- Friends or a person's address
- Laptop
- Makeup kit
- Other medicines

Now every time you pack something in the suitcase, you put a tick mark against the item and then search for what is left in the list. The problem with this method is you are not sure if you have packed everything or if you are simply ticking things off as they come into your mind.

Let's try using a mind map.

In the center, you have your shape that has the words "Workshop Trip" written inside it. Your first branch is "Documents." Under this branch, you will have sub-branches that include your visa, passport, tickets, and other important documents.

Essentially, you are taking one big, disorganized list and creating a sense of order with it. You will have a balloon, square o While making the mind map, I have divided the items. Now, if you must check about what medicines you have to get for the trip, you just need to go to that branch and check.

The map also helps you to further add on some items which you might have missed to write. What if you might need cold cream and sunblock? With a mind map, you not only create a wonderful list, but you also modify an existing list.

How Do Mind Maps Improve Memory?

When you draw, your brain is focused on the task. Mind maps combines drawing with information gathering to allow you to remember pieces of information well. It organizes and structures your thoughts, allowing your brain to avoid complicated and convoluted information presentation. The simpler you make the information for your brain, the easier it becomes for the brain to store it.

Mind maps also promote associations and connections. Association is an important way to improve memory. This is because you are creating connections between different ideas, words, objects, and information, giving your brain more flexibility to work with those connections.

Finally, mind maps use colors and images that stimulate your imagination. This is an essential component to improving the memory.

Teaching Others

What's a good way to learn something? Teach it!

According to research (Koh, Lee & Lim, 2018), teaching allows you to retrieve information better. The reason for this is that you are reinforcing what you learned by relaying it to someone else. Teaching uses repetition, but it also allows your brain to replay the information in a way that makes sense.

Think about it, when you try to teach, you always want to make sure that you are understood. To make that happen, you present the information in the simplest way that you can imagine. Your brain understands this simplicity and goes through the information, arranging it in a cohesive and understandable manner, and we already know how the brain enjoys simplicity.

But what if you're not a teacher? What if you're not part of a classroom? Well, you can imagine one. This may sound like a rather absurd idea, but the brain loves novelty and imagination. They boost the brain's curiosity and ability to store information.

To teach in an imaginary classroom, once you have completed absorbing the information, stand up and pretend you are facing the classroom. It is preferable to stand because motion makes you active, which in turn keeps your brain focused. Once you are ready, start relaying the information as though you are teaching a class. The trick to remember here is that you don't have to sound professional. The most important aspect is the information itself.

Try to speak the information out loud, as clearly as possible. Don't worry if you cannot remember all the facts. Reinforce whatever you can at the moment. Once you are done, go back to the material you have been learning about and see if you have missed any crucial information.

Remember to not simply commit something to memory and then present it. Try to understand the information you are trying to process. When you are "teaching" the information, you shouldn't be simply speaking it out loud, you should be able to explain it. When you are able to explain the information, you create wonderful and new connections in your brain.

Once you have completed your classroom session, give your brain a little break to absorb the information. You can repeat this technique every time you take in new information or if you would like to reinforce old pieces of information. For example, let's say that you had a mental classroom with a piece of complex information. A week later, you can have another teaching session for the same piece of information. However, you should first try and teach without referring to the source material. This allows you to gauge just how much you remember from last time and what you should be focusing on.

Pegword Method

There is a memory technique that you can use to remember numbers or numeric sequences effectively called the Pegword method. The best way to explain the method is by showing how it works. Look at the below rhyme and memorize it:

- One is the sun
- Two is a shoe
- Three is a tree
- Four is the floor
- Five is a hive
- Six is sticks
- Seven is heaven
- Eight is a gate
- Nine is wine
- Ten is a hen

Now, let's say that you have to memorize the number, 7659327. You simply replace the number with the object it signifies. For example, the number seven refers to heaven, six is for sticks, five is connected to a hive, and so on. Once you have given each number a designated object, you can then create a story around the numbers.

For example, you can say that in heaven, there is suddenly a shortage of sticks. And so, you might need to ask the help of a magical bee that lives in a giant beehive. The giant bee asks for wine in return for its help. You realize that there is no more wine for you to offer, but you have heard of a grape tree. And so, you collect the grapes, mash them together using a special shoe and serve it to the bee. The bee gives you the sticks in return, which you promptly bring back to heaven.

Now, why heaven has a shortage of sticks is completely beyond me, but that does not matter. What matters is that you have created this interesting story. Your brain loves the novelty of the story and how unique the entire concept was. Think about it, if you close your eyes right now and try to remember the story I just wrote without having to refer to it again, you might do it really well. You might be surprised that you could remember all the details of the story. But that is exactly what happens when your brain is given the freedom to flex its creativity.

Chapter 9 – The Movie in Your Mind

Imagination is a powerful tool. We have been using it so far in many of the memory techniques that are in this book. But in this chapter, we are going to take it one step further. We are going to use our imaginations to store information.

The Memory Palace

A Memory Palace is a location that you create in your mind. You can use the location to store images that serve as information. However, when I say images, I don't just mean pictures. Even words are a form of image when it comes to the Memory Palace. If you are confused by that statement, you will understand it clearly once we start looking into the technique.

Here is how the technique works:

You start by choosing a location in real life. The location can be your home, office, or the street you live on. However, since we are starting out, we are going to choose your home. Once you have chosen your location, start adding information in different areas of the location. When you want to recollect the information, you simply revisit the location. Sound simple? Let's see how it works in practice.

Step 1: Since we are going to use your home as a location, also called a loci, you are going to imagine that you are at the entrance of your home. You can use any part of your home as a starting point, but the key thing to remember is that you should plan your route in advance in such a way that you can get from point A to point B without going through the same space twice. For this example, I am starting from the entrance and ending my route in the bedroom. But feel free to create your own route.

Step 2: Once you have decided the route, decide what kind of information you would like to memorize. It could be a shopping list, a poem, or a collection of interesting facts.

Step 3: Close your eyes and imagine yourself at the starting point. Place the first items of your list, poem, or collection into that starting point. For example, if you have started your Memory Palace at the entrance to your home and the first item on your shopping list is potatoes, then imagine potatoes right in front of your main door. You can even imagine a board stuck to the entrance with the word "potato" on it.

The kind of mental picture you want to create is entirely up to you but create a vivid and wonderful picture for your brain to remember. If you are remembering entire sentences, then you could imagine them appearing on the door itself or in any other way that you can think up.

Step 4: Now, move to the next point. In the example I have chosen, I will open the main door and step into the hallway of my home. Your second point could be entirely different from mine. Add the next piece of information to the second point. Remember: make it creative and vivid.

Step 5: Head over to the third point and add the third piece of information.

Step 6: Keep doing this until you have finished adding all the pieces of information you need.

Step 7: Once you are done, you can end your Memory Palace or, if you like, you can run through your palace again and check the information you have placed. When you are satisfied, you can open your eyes.

A Memory Palace is a creative way to store information, and it might take a while for your brain to get used to the process. But once you have mastered the technique, it becomes easier to implement. Here are some tips for you to remember when practicing the method:

- Don't worry about the details. Create your Memory Palace to the best of your capabilities. The most important thing for you to focus on is the information.
- You can interact with the objects in the environment. For example, let's say that there is a TV in the living room. You can imagine yourself entering the room, switching on the TV, and seeing the information you are looking for displayed there.

Similarly, you can use other objects in the environment. For example, the photo frames on the walls, the vase in the hallway, the drawers in the kitchen can all hold information. You just have to find creative ways to store your information in those places.

- If you have stored information that you are not going to use immediately, then you can return to your palace to rehearse everything you have stored there. This allows you to see if you would like to add more memory or if you can clearly remember the old ones (which you might want to do when you are beginning to use Memory Palaces).
- The bigger or more detailed the Memory Palace, the more information you can use. This is because you have more points and objects to serve as storage units in your palace.

Mental Cues and How to Create Them

You use cues to help you remember a piece of information that you might have forgotten. Typically, cues are things that we experience using any of our senses. The most common form of cues are reminders that we set on our phone to jolt our memory into remembering the important meeting or getting a carton of milk.

There are two main types of cues that you can use to jolt your memory: internal cues and external cues. Your internal cues are certain patterns of thought that help you trigger a certain memory. For example, if you have lost your keys, then you use mental imagery to imagine the space in your mind and run through a certain set of events. By doing that, you help your brain make connections and help you find your keys. Whereas external cues are events or objects that help you recollect something. For example, keeping a glass of water on your bedside table will remind you to drink water as soon as you wake up.

So, how do you use memory cues?

The first thing that you have to do is find out just what you would like to remind yourself about. Let's say that you would like to remember taking your briefcase with you to a particular meeting. Unfortunately, you have a habit of forgetting your briefcase in the car. How do you solve this problem? You keep an object that you always remember to take with you inside the briefcase. If you are constantly using your mobile phone, then put that into the briefcase. When you forget to take the briefcase and you look for your phone, your memory will snap back to the moment you put the phone in your briefcase. You simply have to find ways to use objects to your advantage and serve as memory cues for you.

Internal memory cues can function in many ways. But one of the best ways to utilize internal cues, especially when you want to recover certain information, is through the Memory Palace. If you have to recollect information, then a Memory Palace will help you recover it when it gets lost.

Now that we have talked about creating imaginative scenarios in our minds and storing information in them, there is something important that we should focus on: How do we take care of our memories? Let's find out in the next chapter.

Chapter 10 – Strong Body, Strong Mind

Taking care of the mind does not mean you neglect the body. In many cases, they are related, and ignoring one might have consequences for the other. According to Mental Health America, exercise and good sleep are important to maintain your mental health (Mental Health America, n.d.). Here are a few ways to keep your body healthy and take care of your mind.

Good Sleep

When you do not have a good sleep, you are unable to learn efficiently. Furthermore, your concentration dwindles and wanders off easily. Your productivity lowers, and you might not manage to go through the exercises mentioned in this book properly.

Let's examine your day-to-day life when you don't get enough sleep. If you have had an unrestful night of sleep, you might find yourself feeling fuzzy, losing the ability to maintain concentration because your eyelids are practically ready to touch each other, or feeling lethargic throughout the day. Sometimes, you might end up struggling to do anything properly. That's not a good sign, especially when you are catching up to deadlines or trying to impress your boss.

In the same way, without the right amount of sleep, you might struggle to maintain your memory. A good sleep is important to make your memory "stick." This is because you are improving the brain's ability to retain information without the effects of sleep deprivation (such as fuzziness) getting in the way.

Healthy Meals

"You are what you eat" is a debatable statement. However, "you live the way you eat" is a statement that cannot be debated. That's because you know, and many doctors have also said, that a good diet is essential for a healthy life.

You should never underestimate what you consume every day. A healthy and balanced meal is the recipe that acts as a therapy for burnt out and stressed lives. When you want to function at an optimal rate, then you need to feed your body with "good fuel." Add in those fresh fruits and vegetables, minimize cholesterol intake, keep away harmful fats, and make sure that you don't overindulge on high sugar and high calorie foods.

Let's think of it this way. If you would like to keep your car's engine running smoothly, then you are going to make sure that you use a good fuel. You are not going to add grease into your tank now, are you?

All the bad stuff you eat. That's the grease for your body's fuel tank.

Fresh Air

To take advantage of fresh air, make sure you know how to breathe it in properly. You might think to yourself that you have always been breathing air properly. But too often, we are stressed out in our lives because of our work, life challenges, or relationships. We don't focus on heading out and are simply inhaling a lungful of fresh air.

Make sure that you are not in areas of constant pollution. Try and improve the air quality in offices and homes if required. But, if you are thinking about investing in that air purifier, that is not what I am talking about. What I mean is that you should allow some fresh air to enter your office or home space.

If you don't have enough or any windows to help you with ventilation, then take a step outside whenever you get the chance. And if you find yourself in a busy part of the city where the air might have a high degree of pollutants, then make sure that you are giving yourself time to venture out into a part of the city where you can experience some fresh air.

Get Physical!

Almost everyone in the world can agree that exercise is good for us. Without it, our body begins to slow down and weaken more quickly. This affects various parts of the body, including the brain. And when the brain gets affected, well then you can kiss that memory goodbye.

Try and have a 30-minute session of exercise most days of the week. You don't have to lift weights to create a body that can deflect arrows. You simply have to make sure that you are at least taking a brisk walk or, even better, jogging. Even on a daily basis, if you find yourself sitting in one position for a long period of time, then get up and move around. Do not allow your body to remain inactive for a long period of time.

Smoking and Drinking

Finally, we come to substances that many people consume on a regular basis but do not realize how it affects them in more ways than one. While the research on the effects of smoking on memory is still ongoing, it is clear that cigarettes contribute towards the breakdown of certain parts of the brain. This could involve the parts that are focused on memory.

When it comes to drinking, everyone knows how it can affect short-term memory. However, frequent consumption may have long-term effects as well (Leutieri, 2019). We are not talking about the fact that you might not remember what happened the previous night. We are talking about the fact that you might start having problems remembering various bits of information for the rest of your life.

Benefits of Exercise on the Mind

Your brain functions similar to other muscles in the body. The more you use it, the more you improve it. So far, we have been looking at numerous mental exercises that are important to keep your brain active. But what about physical exercises?

According to research published by the University of Georgia (Tomporowski, 2003), physical exercises can actually boost memory capabilities and processing. But, how is this possible?

One of the things that takes place when you exercise is your heart rate increases. Increased heart rate means that more blood is pumping throughout your body, including your brain. At the same time, your body becomes more active. It starts producing all the necessary hormones for you to perform in peak condition.

Exercises also improve brain plasticity. When your brain is allowed to expand, it can create better neural connections. This allows you to store memories better, since now you have more connections to work with.

Further, exercise helps reduce stress levels in the body. When your body is pumped full of stress, then it becomes distracting for the brain since it now has to focus on preventing the stress levels from overloading your system. It does not have the capacity to focus on anything else other than making things better for you. Physical activity acts like a drainage system for your stress, allowing it to drain away from your body.

But as we talk about the benefits of exercise, we often wonder about something else. Just what kind of exercises should we be doing to improve our memory? Here are some tips to follow when choosing the right exercise.

Tips on Exercises to Keep the Brain Healthy

- Typically, choose any exercise that is good for your heart. It will help the brain improve as well.

- Choose aerobic exercises as they improve your brain function and help your body repair brain cells. Some of the aerobic exercises that you can use are swimming, running, rowing, and boxing.
- Have you stumbled across mental blocks or feel mentally exhausted? Then jumping jacks are simple exercises you can perform to improve your brain's stamina, allowing it to function longer and clearing away any mental blocks.
- If you feel like changing your exercises, look for an activity that brings together cardiovascular exercises and coordination, such as Zumba or dance classes.
- If you like spending time at the gym, then focus on circuit workouts. One example of a circuit workout would be to start with push-ups, then move to sit-ups, squats, chin-ups, and lunges. You can also try circuit workouts at home or at the gym. Here are a few options.
    - Option 1: Jump ropes, jumping jacks, body weight squats, lunges
    - Option 2: Push-ups, walking

lunges, plank, jumping jacks
- Option 3: One-legged squats, body weight squats, walking lunges

Sleep and Memory

Getting a good night's sleep makes you feel better. Your body recharges and your brain feels refreshed when you wake up in the morning. But sleep also contributes to a healthy memory.

When you are sleeping, your brain is active. It is arranging all the information and ideas that you have collected during the day in the form of memories. If you are sleep deprived, then you impair your ability to store information properly.

You have seen the three stages of memory: encoding, storage, and recall. The encoding and recall process happens when you are awake. After all, you won't be using any memories when you are asleep. Which leaves the storage part? When does this happen?

You guess it. During your sleep.

Regardless of what kind of memory you are trying to store, you will need adequate sleep so that your brain can do its job. If you don't have proper sleep, then your brain might do a haphazard job of organizing memories.

Have you ever been in a situation where you wake up the next morning, feeling drowsy from the lack of sleep, and unable to focus? You realize that it is suddenly much more difficult to remember things, but you think that perhaps a good cup of coffee might help you get your brain back in the game. The truth is that while you can boost your brain slightly with the caffeine, you are looking at poor performance in the long run. This means that you might give a little mental kick to your brain in the morning. But by the afternoon, you are looking for a bed or a sofa to nap.

Not only has your brain not stored all the information, but it is dealing with new information as well. Let's imagine that you have to organize items for a picnic. You are storing in some snacks in bags when you accidentally knock over the bags, spilling the snacks on the floor. Luckily, they are all covered in plastic wrap, but you dread the fact that you have to organize them all over again.

Taking a deep sigh, you decide that you better get it over with. Unfortunately, you notice the time on the clock and realize that there are so many other tasks to do. You hurriedly start stuffing the snacks into the bag, not bothering to check their condition. In your state of panic, you leave some of the snacks on the ground while you handle another task. The result is that you are looking at a very disorganized plan.

The same scenario plays out with your brain. It has hardly finished putting the memories in the proper place when you have to wake up and go about your day. In the process, there are pending memories to arrange. Before you know it, the brain is busy trying to help you focus as you make your way to the subway, get into the train, get out at your stop, and make your way to the office. It tries to keep you as attentive as possible so that you are dealing with all the situations happening around you properly. So, It is important to allow the brain to deal with what it has at the moment. And the one way to do that is to give it proper sleep.

Scientists are not exactly certain how sleep and memories are related, but the most common theory has to do with the hippocampus. This part of the brain reviews and organizes memories. One research also held that your dreams are a result of your brain arranging your memories. Which is why some of your dreams appear so vivid. For example, let's say that you learned some interesting facts about tigers during your day and also planned out your boating trip with friends. That night, you might dream about tigers walking on water, which happens because your brain is dealing with the tiger and boating trip information at the same time.

In this day and age, it is quite difficult to get a good night's sleep. So, here are some tips on getting good rest:

- Make sure that you head to bed and wake up at the same time every day. This let's your body know when to prepare itself for memory consolidation and arrangement.
- Do not exercise close to bedtime. Your body becomes pumped with adrenaline and that only serves to keep you more awake.

- Do not have caffeine, nicotine, or alcohol before going to sleep. In fact, avoid caffeine after 6 pm.
- If you feel that you might have difficulty sleeping or if you have too many things on your mind, then try and unwind for a while. You can meditate, read a book, take a warm bath, or listen to some relaxing music.
- Have your meals at least 2 to 3 hours prior to sleeping.

Conclusion

The memory is a complex construct that is part of an even more complex construct: your brain. Today, we know a lot more about memory than we had before, but the information we have gathered still does not paint a complete picture.

There is much work to be done in the field of memory research. Take for example the case of the woman who had half her brain removed, but still went on to become a speech pathologist (Wheat, 2016). If someone had told psychologists that it would be possible to function fairly normally with just half their brains, they would think that someone might have possibly lost half their own brain. Yet the reality cannot be ignored. It is possible and it has happened to someone. This goes to show that the more we think we know about the brain, the more mysteries we uncover. The same goes for our memory.

Today, we know that neurons in our brains create connections that result in memories. The more connections that these neurons create, the strong the memory is. And here's the kicker: neurons are created in the gut as well. Pretty surprising, isn't it? Our body has always been brimming with secrets to unearth.

What we know so far allows us to work on our memory. It gives us the knowledge to change not only our ideas about memory, but memory itself. And you know what they say about knowledge having power.

We have the power to change the way our memory functions. We can make differences to the way information gets stored in our brains and the effectiveness of their recollection. In this book, you dived into the inner workings of your mind. You understand how your mental processes work, you have been introduced to the basics of memory, you have learned about brain waves and memory preferences, and you have looked at various mental exercises and techniques to take care of your body.

You entered the mindset of a memory genius to try and incorporate the same mindset into your life. You have also learned how the brain forgets certain memories in order to make space for new ones. As you discovered more about information overload, you realized that it is essential to feed your brain the right kind of information, the kind that is beneficial to you.

All of these are the ways in which you can improve your memory. By practicing the techniques in this book and using them in your life as well, you are training your brain to become a master at encoding, retention, and recollection.

If I have to leave you with one key piece of advice, then it would be this: Do not let disappointments stop your progress. Remember that just because you don't see immediate results does not mean that no changes are occurring. You are likely introducing the brain to a whole new set of rules, ideas, and practices.

It won't be easy for your grey and white matter to adapt easily. However, as you practice, the changes might become more obvious to you. Keep challenging yourself so that you can improve even more.

Stay sharp. Stay focused. Most of all, I hope you reach the memory goals that you have set for yourself.

The end... almost!

Reviews are not easy to come by.

As an independent author with a tiny marketing budget, I rely on readers, like you, to leave a short review on Amazon.

Even if it's just a sentence or two!

So if you enjoyed the book, please leave a review.

I am very appreciative for your review as it truly makes a difference.

Thank you from the bottom of my heart for purchasing this book and reading it to the end.

References

Chawla, D. (2018). To Remember, the Brain Must Actively Forget. Retrieved from https://www.quantamagazine.org/to-remember-the-brain-must-actively-forget-20180724/

Christakis, N., & Fowler, J. (2011). *Connected.* New York: Little, Brown.

Deleon, N. (2009). Study: Americans consume 34 gigabytes of information per day – TechCrunch. Retrieved from https://techcrunch.com/2009/12/09/study-americans-consume-34-gigabytes-of-information-per-day/

Dresler, M., Shirer, W., Konrad, B., Müller, N., Wagner, I., & Fernández, G. et al. (2017). Mnemonic Training Reshapes Brain Networks to Support Superior Memory. Neuron, 93(5), 1227-1235.e6. doi: 10.1016/j.neuron.2017.02.003

Ghose, T. (2016). The Human Brain's Memory Could Store the Entire Internet. Retrieved from https://www.livescience.com/53751-brain-could-store-internet.html

Hasselmo, M. (2006). The role of acetylcholine in learning and memory. Current Opinion In Neurobiology, 16(6), 710-715. doi: 10.1016/j.conb.2006.09.002

Koh, A., Lee, S., & Lim, S. (2018). The learning benefits of teaching: A retrieval practice hypothesis. Applied Cognitive Psychology, 32(3), 401-410. doi: 10.1002/acp.3410

Mental Health America. (n.d.). Care For Your Health. Retrieved from https://www.mentalhealthamerica.net/care-your-health

Napier, N. (2014). The Myth of Multitasking. Retrieved from https://www.psychologytoday.com/intl/blog/creativity-without-borders/201405/the-myth-multitasking

Liu, W., Ge, T., Leng, Y., Pan, Z., Fan, J., Yang, W., & Cui, R. (2017). The Role of Neural Plasticity in Depression: From Hippocampus to

Prefrontal Cortex. Neural Plasticity, 2017, 1-11. doi: 10.1155/2017/6871089

Maguire, E., Woollett, K., & Spiers, H. (2006). London taxi drivers and bus drivers: A structural MRI and neuropsychological analysis. Hippocampus, 16(12), 1091-1101. doi: 10.1002/hipo.20233

Pearsall, P., Schwartz, G., & Russek, L. (2000). Changes in heart transplant recipients that parallel the personalities of their donors. Integrative Medicine, 2(2-3), 65-72. doi: 10.1016/s1096-2190(00)00013-5

Rettner, R. (2019). Fetuses Have Memories. Retrieved from https://www.livescience.com/5585-fetuses-memories.html

Tomporowski, P. (2003). Effects of acute bouts of exercise on cognition. Acta Psychologica, 112(3), 297-324. doi: 10.1016/s0001-6918(02)00134-8

Underwood, E. (2019). New neurons for life? Old people can still make fresh brain cells, study finds. Retrieved from https://www.sciencemag.org/news/2019/03/ne

w-neurons-life-old-people-can-still-make-fresh-brain-cells-study-finds

Wheat, A. (2016). Woman Who Had Half Her Brain Removed Defies the Odds, Gets a Master's Degree. Retrieved https://people.com/celebrity/woman-who-had-half-her-brain-removed-defies-the-odds-gets-a-masters-degree/